D0553577

STUDIES IN HEBREWS

Studies in Hebrews

HERSCHEL H. HOBBS

SUNDAY SCHOOL BOARD
SOUTHERN BAPTIST CONVENTION

NASHVILLE, TENNESSEE

PRINTED IN THE UNITED STATES OF AMERICA
225.MY54RRD

To
MY MOTHER
who "having obtained a good report
through faith"
has received her "promise."

Contents

The Sunday School Training Course

THE SUNDAY SCHOOL TRAINING COURSE prepared by the Sunday School Department of the Baptist Sunday School Board is one of the major means of promoting Sunday school work. Its influence is limited only by its use.

The six sections of the course include studies in Bible, doctrines, evangelism, Sunday school leadership and administration, teaching, age group studies, and special studies. The range of the course is broad, for the field of Sunday school work is broad and requires comprehensive and specific training. Sixteeen books are required for the completion of each Diploma.

The study of the training course is not to be limited to the present Sunday school workers. Most churches need twice as many workers as are now enlisted. This need can be supplied by training additional workers now. Members of the Young People's and Adult classes and older Intermediates should be led to study these books, for thereby will their service be assured. Parents will find help as they study what the Sunday school is trying to do.

SPECIAL NOTE TO INSTRUCTORS:

During your teaching of this book will you check with the Sunday school superintendent and see if an accurate record of training for the workers is kept. If not, please urge him to set up such a file with an associate superintendent of training in charge. File cards for this purpose may be ordered at nominal cost from your nearest Baptist Book Store.

J. N. BARNETTE

Secretary, Sunday School Department
Baptist Sunday School Board

Directions for the Teaching and Study of This Book for Credit

I. DIRECTIONS FOR THE TEACHER

1. Ten class periods of forty-five minutes each, or the equivalent, are required for the completion of a book for credit.

2. The teacher is given an award on the book taught when he requests it.

3. The teacher shall give a written examination covering the subject matter in the textbook. The examination may take the form of assigned work to be done between the class sessions, in the class sessions, or as a final examination.

EXCEPTION: All who attend all of the class sessions; who read the book through by the close of the course; and who, in the judgment of the teacher, do the class-work satisfactorily may be exempted from taking the examination.

4. Either Sunday school or Training Union credit (*to Young People and Adults only in Training Union*) may be had for the study of this book. Application for Sunday school awards should be sent to the state Sunday school department, for Training Union awards to the state Training Union department, where forms may be secured on which to make application. These forms should be made in triplicate. Keep the last copy for the church file, and send the other two copies.

II. DIRECTIONS FOR THE STUDENT*

(* *The student must be fifteen years of age or older to receive Sunday school credit. Training Union credit on this book is not granted to Juniors and Intermediates.*)

1. *In Classwork*

(1) The student must attend at least six of the ten forty-five minute class periods to be entitled to take the class examination.

(2) The student must certify that the textbook has been read. (In rare cases where students may find it impracticable to read the book before the completion of the classwork, the teacher may accept a promise to read the book carefully within the next two weeks. This applies only to students who do written work.)

(3) The student must take a written examination, making a minimum grade of 70 per cent, or qualify according to *Exception* noted above.

2. *In Individual Study by Correspondence*

Those who for any reason wish to study the book without the guidance of a teacher will use one of the following methods:

(1) Write answers to the questions printed in the book, or

(2) Write a development of the chapter outlines.

In either case the student must read the book through.

Students may find profit in studying the text together, but where awards are requested, individual papers are required.

All written work done by such students on books for Sunday school credit should be sent to the state Sunday school secretary. All of such work done on books for Training Union credit should be sent to the state Training Union secretary.

NOTE.—*This book is in Section I of the Sunday School Training Course.*

Introduction

WHEN THE REQUEST came that I undertake to write *Studies in Hebrews*, my heart was filled with a twofold joy: because we were going to study this epistle, and because I was to have the privilege of writing the guidebook for the study. Since assuming this responsibility, I have asked many pastors how much use they make of the Epistle of the Hebrews. Most have said that their use of it is largely confined to a few isolated texts. It is well that we are about to rediscover this vital portion of the Scriptures.

The reader will discover that we have sought to derive from the epistle that which makes it vital to twentieth-century Christianity. In so doing, we feel that we have found that which made it important in the first century—and since. As it was written to Christian people with a Hebrew background, we would expect to find its meaning in the light of their former history. For that reason, in every instance we have sought to form a contact with the author's own thoughts by relating his literary work to the particular instance in Hebrew history which he had in mind. Apart from that background we cannot understand the picture which he paints.

One cannot hope to cover in so brief a volume the entire span of truth contained in Hebrews. However, if we have pointed out some avenues of thought over which we may travel toward a better understanding of God's eternal purpose—then our efforts will have been fully rewarded.

May God's Holy Spirit illumine our minds, breathe upon our spirits, and make pliable our wills as we apply ourselves not only to an understanding of—but to an undertaking in—the redemptive will of God for his people.

STUDIES IN HEBREWS

1

THE PREVIEW OF
THE PROBLEM

IN THE Epistle to the Hebrews we stand at the watershed of the religious experience of the human race. From that vantage point the author enables us to catch a panoramic view of God's eternal purpose of redemption. Looking back through the Old Testament, we catch a glimpse of the tiny rill of God's purpose as it bursts forth from the fountain of God's redemptive love. Gradually it broadens and deepens into a mighty river winding its life-giving way through the pages of ancient history only to lose itself in the dry desert sands of a disobedient people. Presently in Christ we see it emerge as a fountain of living water, springing up into eternal life and causing the desert of unredeemed souls to blossom as a rose. Looking forward in the New Testament and beyond, we see it as "a pure river of water of life, clear as crystal, proceeding out of the throne of God and of the Lamb" (Rev. 22:1), coursing its redemptive way through all ages and to all peoples. Into its swelling current we are urged to launch our ships of faith, that through our witness, the knowledge of God shall cover the earth as the waters cover the sea.

Against this background let us turn to an examination of the Epistle to the Hebrews. There is no other book in the New Testament which presents more unsettled problems. We cannot be certain as to its title. We do not know the name of the author. We cannot be dogmatic as to its date. Its place of origin is disputed as vehemently as its destination and recipients. There is a widespread difference of opinion among scholars as to its purpose. Why, then, do we propose to study it at all? In the first place, these very problems challenge and intrigue us. They are vital in our understanding of the epistle. In the second place, the epistle is of infinite value as a religious document. It presents to us the most exalted picture of Christ to be found anywhere in the holy Scriptures. Furthermore, it involves for every Christian a timeless goal and challenge as to the meaning of his spiritual experience. While modern scholars may differ as to the questions raised above, they are united in the conviction that the writing is inspired Scripture and deserves its place in the sacred canon.

I.   THE PROBLEM OF TITLE AND STYLE

The title most familiar to the average reader is that given by the King James Version as "the Epistle of Paul the Apostle to the Hebrews." We may safely say that modern scholarship has challenged every word in this traditional title. Suffice it to say that it does not appear in any of the oldest manuscripts. It was probably added at a later date by some copyist as the Pauline authorship became accepted by the churches.

According to the most ancient manuscripts the title was simply "To Hebrews." While some modern scholars question its originality, the weight of literary evidence seems to tip the scales in its favor.

The style of the epistle is important for our understanding of its message. Someone has aptly said that it begins like a treatise, proceeds like a sermon, and ends like a letter. Despite the claims of some to the contrary, the epistle gives every evidence of being a unit. It shows evidence of a studied rhetoric, without "the impetuous eloquence of Paul." Dr. Adolf Deissmann suggests that Hebrews marks an epoch in the history of the Christian religion, indicating that it has begun "to lay hands on the instruments of culture; the literary and theological period has begun."

II. THE PROBLEM OF AUTHORSHIP

Who wrote the epistle? Eusebius quotes Origen as replying, "God only knows." Someone has fittingly added that God has not chosen to speak regarding it. Certainly the epistle itself, like the Fourth Gospel, is silent on the subject. But if silence has reigned in these areas, it has certainly been dethroned elsewhere. To mention a few names, the epistle has variously been assigned to Paul, Barnabas, Apollos, Peter, Luke, Priscilla and Aquila, Silas, Philip the Deacon, Aristion, and Clement of Rome. The most ancient and persistent theories as to the authorship of Hebrews center about Paul and Barnabas. Martin Luther attributed it to Apollos, and Dr. A. T. Robertson offers the "guess" that he was most likely correct. Many scholars since Luther's day have followed his position. Space forbids a thorough discussion of this problem. In short, we may rather safely say that the results of modern scholarship tend to eliminate Paul as the probable author. If neither Barnabas nor Apollos wrote Hebrews, it must have been someone like them. A good case can be made for either. For myself I should choose Barnabas, but one cannot be dogmatic.

III. THE PROBLEM OF DATE

Again we find wide disagreement among the scholars. Dates all the way from A.D. 50 to A.D. 96 have been suggested. However, at least six factors may be considered in determining a probable date.

First, we know that Hebrews could not have been

written later than A.D. 95, for about that time Clement of Rome made use of it in his letter to Corinth. Second, some have suggested a later date within this period on the basis that its readers were those who had been converted by the Lord's personal disciples. However, we are not required to suppose any great length of time for this to have taken place. Third, it has been pointed out that the doctrinal development calls for a time somewhere between the later Pauline epistles, for example, Colossians (about A.D. 63), and the Johannine writings (A.D. 80-95). Paul was martyred in A.D. 68; John wrote from about A.D. 80 onward; Hebrews could have followed closely upon the former event and some time before the latter period.

Fourth, the epistle makes mention of the fact that its readers have endured persecution and continue to do so (10:33ff.; 12:4). If we suppose the ordeal to be widespread, we might fasten on to the persecution under Nero, A.D. 64–68, or the one under Domitian after A.D. 81. A better case can be made in favor of the earlier date. Fifth, the mention of Timothy's liberation from prison (13:23) throws some light upon the problem. Paul urged Timothy to come to Rome shortly before his death in A.D. 68 (2 Tim. 4:11-13, 21). We may suppose that he came and was imprisoned. Some time after the death of Nero on June 8, A.D. 68 he may well have been released. This could have happened in the latter part of that year or the early part of the next. This would put us somewhere near A.D. 69. Sixth, many scholars regard the fall of Jerusalem in A.D. 70 as a pivotal point in fixing the date. The author does not mention this catastrophe. He does seem to indicate that the Temple and its sacrificial system are still in existence (10:1ff.), but that they are "ready to vanish away" (8:13). This would seem to indicate a time in the latter part of the Jewish War, say A.D. 68–70.

Summarizing the evidence, we find that we are confined to a date somewhere between A.D. 50 and A.D. 95. The religious development of the readers does not require a date more than thirty or forty years beyond Pentecost, which would leave us somewhere in the period from A.D. 60 to A.D. 70. The doctrinal content of the epistle would fit this period. Such a period would bring us into the atmosphere of the Neronic persecution of A.D. 64–68. Timothy's liberation from prison could well fall into the A.D. 68–69 period, probably the latter year. The Jerusalem temple is still standing but is ready to vanish away. It actually was destroyed in A.D. 70. The year prior to that cataclysmic event would fit the author's statement. Therefore we may with confidence set A.D. 69 as the probable date of writing for Hebrews.

IV. THE PROBLEM OF DESTINATION

Here again we are confronted with an insoluble problem. Jerusalem, Antioch, Rome, Alexandria, Colosse, Ephesus, Berea, even Ravenna, and others have been suggested. Until the nineteenth century Palestine, or Jerusalem, was generally accepted as the destination. Since then Alexandria in Egypt has been offered as the recipient of the epistle. More recently Rome has come in for consideration.

The truth of the matter is—we do not know. The individual's own judgment will have the final word. About all that we can say with certainty is that Hebrews was written to a congregation of Hebrew Christians, large or small, somewhere. The value of the epistle does not depend upon our knowledge of its destination. This uncertainty may even add to the universal application of its timeless truths. The author of Hebrews gives warning to those who are not Christians and assurance to all those who have accepted the Lord.

V. The Problem of Purpose

What was the author's purpose in writing Hebrews? Some have entertained the idea that it was written as a warning to those who had not yet become Christians and who were on the verge of turning back without believing. However, the historical position to which the majority of Bible scholars both past and present adhere is that the epistle was written to Hebrew Christians who had had a genuine experience of grace, but who were faced with the temptation of forsaking Christianity to return to Judaism. Even among this group there is a wide difference of opinion as to the cause of this tendency. It is quite clear from the text itself that they were enduring heavy persecution, perhaps from the Roman government.

Beyond this evident fact there is a multiplicity of positions. Some find the temptation rooted in the impending destruction of the Temple in Jerusalem with its attendant doubts to which immature Hebrew Christians would be susceptible. Others detect evidence of disappointment on the part of these young Christians over the low moral standards and gross spiritual ignorance on the part of Gentile Christians. Still others find the cause in the readers' disappointment over the postponement of our Lord's promised return. More recently there comes the suggestion that their danger was not of a relapse into Judaism but a loss of the significance of their Christian profession due to their continuing to live under the shadow of Jewish legalism.

Quite naturally one hesitates to take issue with such an array of intellects as are represented in the aforementioned positions. However, we believe that a thorough study of the epistle reveals a deeper underlying purpose than any or all of the ideas included in the above. Quite naturally we would not claim to be saying the final word on the many problems found in Hebrews. Many competent scholars will no doubt disagree with the position which we have taken with regard to the epistle. If we are in error, we trust that others will correct us. However, if our efforts throw any light whatever upon this marvelous portion of Holy Writ, our efforts will not have been in vain.

In my humble judgment we have magnified the author's arguments to the loss of his thesis. While Hebrews gives to us one of the most exalted pictures of Christ to be found in the Bible, the author's primary purpose was not to deal in Christology. He glorifies Christ and his redemptive ministry only as the basis upon which to project his purpose. The truth of the matter is that Hebrews is more of a written sermon than it is a letter. It is perfectly outlined and eloquently written. As such we should expect to find the author's purpose not so much in his argument as in his application of the argument. In at least five places throughout the epistle (2:1ff.; 3:7ff.; 6:1ff.; 10:19ff.; 12:1ff.) he turns aside from presenting his evidence in order to exhort his readers to act in the light of it.

Naturally if we start out with the wrong premise, our conclusion will be wrong. Through the centuries a vast body of Christianity has held to the belief, unsupported by the New Testament, that one can be saved and then lost again. This has led to the introduction into our language of the word "apostasy," which means to forsake one's God or religion. We shall see that this word is not a translation but a transliteration of the Greek word *apostasia,* which in turn comes from the verb *apostēnai.* We shall see later that this word has a root meaning far removed from its English cousin. A kindred example of this is the case of our failure to translate the Greek word *baptizō,* meaning to dip, plunge, or immerse. Instead of translating it, pedo-Baptist scholars transliterate it as *baptize,* and leave to the reader's own belief the task of supplying its meaning. The result is the body of error which is related to the ordinance of baptism.

In the writer's opinion we have gone astray in transliterating the word *apostēnai,* with the result that the entire Epistle to the Hebrews is regarded as a warning against apostasy in the modern sense of the word. Those who, on the basis of other New Testament passages, deny the possibility of apostasy seek to get around the difficulty by simply saying that the author uses the idea of apostasy as a hypothetical case which cannot really happen. If so, then why use it?

No, the answer is elsewhere. Treating the various passages in question, we have sought in dealing with such phrases as "let them slip" (2:1), "evil heart of unbelief, in departing from the living God" (3:12), "if they shall fall away" (6:6), "if we sin wilfully," etc. (10:26), and kindred ideas, to *let the Bible say what it says.* We shall reserve our discussion of these until we come to them naturally in our study of the text itself.

Suffice it to say that the purpose of the author in writing this wonderful epistle is to issue a clarion call to Christian people of every age to go on in the fulfilment of their part in God's redemptive purpose or world mission.[1] The sum and substance of the message of the epistle is that in every age God has redeemed a people through whom to declare his message to a lost world. Failure on the part of a people, both individually and collectively,

---

[1] Note that W. H. Griffith Thomas' *Let Us Go On* (Zondervan) deals with "the secret of Christian progress in the Epistle to the Hebrews." After completing the manuscript, I was delighted to see that William Manson's *The Epistle to the Hebrews* (Hodder and Stoughton) arrives at the general idea of "the world-mission of Christianity," although his approach is somewhat different.

to fit into this purpose results in their rejection in favor of another. In that light, for our own satisfaction, at least, every difficult passage in the epistle becomes clear. Furthermore, this purpose permeates even the comparison between Judaism and Christianity. The consequence of Israel's failure in the light of her privilege foretells a greater consequence in the event of failure on the part of Christian people in the light of their great privilege.

Against this background we shall see that the original readers of the epistle, while genuine Christians, were suffering from a state of arrested development in their divine calling, which was further aggravated by the hostility of the world about them. Like so many today, they were content simply to be redeemed from sin, with no concern for the will of God for them or for the plight of others who know not God in Christ. They were overlooking the fact that a full salvation included redemption—plus a continuing growth in grace and service which ultimately evolves into a Christian character made in the image of God. The author thus issues to them his challenge both negatively and positively; negatively, as he exhorts them to avoid the failure of Israel and, positively, as he presents to them the glorious person and power of Christ, our ally or "partner" in God's redemptive plan. *His challenge has nothing whatever to do with apostasy into Judaism.* The crusading call of the author is not "Don't go back!"—but "Let us go on!" (6:1).

It is this very fact which makes Hebrews so vital to us today. It has been largely a neglected book. What appeal does the traditional interpretation have for modern Christians? We are in no danger of apostatizing into Judaism. True, we face temptation to fraternize with the world. But that is another matter. On the other hand, if the message of Hebrews is a call to a world mission,

then it is as fresh as though the first ink on the original
was yet undried.

It is in this light that we approach the study of this
wonderful epistle. In it is the most tremendous message
for our age—and for every age.

FOR REVIEW AND FURTHER STUDY

1.   What is the oldest title ascribed to the epistle?
2.   Name some of the reputed authors of Hebrews? Who
     was Barnabas?
3.   What six factors must we consider in determining
     the date of Hebrews?
4.   What three cities are the most probable destination
     of the epistle?
5.   What is the traditional view regarding the purpose
     of Hebrews? Give the purpose which is suggested by
     the author of *Studies in Hebrews*.

2

THE WORD FROM
THE ETERNAL

[1:1 to 2:18]

GOD SPAKE . . ." is the ringing note of Hebrews. In writing to Hebrew Christians it is natural that the author of Hebrews would form a common ground by declaring the fact of divine revelation and by recognizing Judaism as the fruit of such. Furthermore, it is to be expected that, in keeping with his thesis, he would point beyond that which was good to something which is better. If Judaism was the result of a good revelation, Christianity is the fruit of a better one. In view of this fact it naturally follows that under this better revelation more is to be expected of those who espouse it. To implement this idea, he points out the ultimate purpose of all divine revelation to which his readers should aspire.

I. THE ELEMENTS IN REVELATION (1:1-14)

1. *The Divine Element (1:1a)*

The source of all revelation is God. The author does not argue for his existence, he merely assumes that he is (cf. Gen. 1:1; John 1:1). He also assumes that God reveals himself. Since the essential nature of God is love, he can do no other than manifest himself to those who believe in him.

God is not discovered; he reveals himself. Man's knowledge of God is not derived from his upward and laborious climb from the valley of polytheism to the pinnacle of monotheism. Neither is God a mere projection of man's personality, as some claim; he is the Person from whom man receives all that is highest and noblest in his being (Gen. 2:7). In one word—"God"—the author of Hebrews sets aside the machinations of those who seek to discover the origin and goal of true religion amid the blind gropings of sinful men. He declares them to be given through the self-unveiling of a mighty and merciful God.

Furthermore, he declares that this revelation is personal. While God is evidenced in the work of his hands (Psalm 8), he reveals himself by the word of his mouth. By the work of his hands God could show his majesty and might. But only through an interplay of his personality with the personality of man could he demonstrate his love and mercy. The end result of the revelation of God is his salvation worked out in man—full, complete, and purposeful salvation.

2. *The Human Element (1:1b)*

We are further reminded that while revelation is divine, its object and means "in times past" are human. God revealed himself to man ("fathers") through man ("prophets"). While he does not specifically say it, we are reminded that "God . . . spake" as "holy men of God . . . were moved [picked up and borne along] by the Holy Ghost" (2 Peter 1:21). But the emphasis here is upon the human element in revelation.

In so doing the author declares that the Old Testament is a revelation from God. Through Noah, Abraham, Moses, David, and the prophets he has spoken to the fathers in time past. By dreams, visions, signs, in spoken voice, and in "divers manners" God has revealed his will to men. Using instruments from men to mules, he has unveiled himself. But always his revelation was through imperfect instruments.

Of necessity this revelation was fragmentary and incomplete. "At sundry times" is more aptly translated "in many portions." Thus we are reminded of the progressive nature of God's revelation. This is not to say that God's ability to reveal himself was limited. Rather it refers to man's inability to receive the revelation. The ocean is not limited by the teacup in man's hand; but man's ability to receive it is so limited. God could of necessity reveal himself only as man was enabled to comprehend it. We find more of God in John than in Genesis, but the God of the one is the God of the other. The difference is in man. In the latter, man is in the kindergarten; in the former, he is in graduate school. To say that God's progressive revelation is due to his weakness rather than to that of man would be no more foolish than the child who on promotion day said to his teacher, "My! I wish you knew enough to teach me in the second grade!"

Obviously, then, while the Old Testament Scriptures are the revelation of God, they are not his final word to man. The imperfection of his media and the consequently fragmentary character of his message imply that there is more. It is this truth that the author avows in the opening statement of the epistle.

3. *The Human-divine Element (1:2-14)*

Since revelation is divine in source and human in means, it is to be expected that the perfect revelation would be through One who was both human and divine. The author moves naturally to this truth as he declares that God who "spake in time past . . . by the prophets, hath in these last days spoken unto us by his [a] Son." The word "spake" in the original is an aorist participle, "having spoken," suggesting the incomplete nature of the former revelation. "Hath spoken" is an aorist indicative of the same verb, "did speak," indicating the final and full revelation through the Son. The word "Son" is the key thought here. In the original it is without the definite article. He is "a Son" in contrast to "the prophets." The emphasis is on *what* he is rather than on *who* he is. Later (4:14) this Son will be identified with Jesus, the human-divine Son of God. In short, he is not a mere vehicle of revelation, but he is God in human form revealing himself (John 14:9). His revelation is not fragmentary but complete; not partial but perfect; not preparatory but ultimate. The revelation is perfect in essence; but due to man's inability it is yet imperfect in comprehension (John 16:12).

To emphasize the superiority of the new revelation over the old, the author points out seven (a perfect number) ways in which the Son is superior to those through whom God had spoken "in time past." Being "appointed heir of all things" (v. 2), he is the *Goal* toward which all creation moves. He is the *Creator* "by whom also he [God] made the worlds" (v. 2). He is the Alpha and the Omega, the beginning and the end (Rev. 1:8). As the brightness of his glory and "the express image of his person" (v. 3), he is the *exact Image* of God, the perfect expression of his character from eternity. He is not of like substance but is the same substance with God (John 1:1; Phil. 2:6; Col. 1:15). From eternity to eternity he is the *Sustainer* of the universe, "upholding all things by the word of his power" (v. 3; cf. Col. 1:17). He is our *Redeemer,* having "himself purged our sins" (v. 3). The reference is to the climax of his incarnate revelation of God as Saviour. He is both the Revealer of God and the Redeemer of man. He is our *King* who, following his redemptive work, "sat down on the right hand of the

Majesty on high" (v. 3; cf. Phil. 2:7-11). As our Prophet, Priest, and King (v. 3), he is *exalted above the angels* (vv. 4ff). There can be no stronger expression than these concerning the deity of Christ.

Enlarging upon this thought regarding angels, we are reminded that the revelation through Christ is "better" (v. 4) than the law of Moses which the Jews regarded as being given through angels (Acts 7:38, 53). This truth is driven home with a sixfold comparison of the Son and angels. While the angels are servants of God (v. 7) and of the heirs of salvation (v. 14), the Son possesses Sonship (v. 5); he is worshiped by angels (v. 6); is a King (v. 8); is the anointed One (v. 9); is the Creator (vv. 10-12); and possesses rulership (vv. 13f).

Therefore in the author's examination of divine revelation we see the superiority of the Christian revelation over that of Judaism. The former does not destroy the latter but completes it. Both the Old Testament and the New Testament have God for their source. The one is given in progressive portions through inferior instruments. The other is one full expression of the human-divine Son of God. The one is partial and temporary; the other is complete and final. Ultimately God has spoken in a Son and has no other word for man.

II. THE NEGLECT OF DIVINE REVELATION (2:1-4)

1. *The Problem of Neglect (2:1)*

Here we have the first of five exhortations which are injected throughout the epistle. These passages are perhaps some of the most difficult for interpretation in the entire Bible. The problem of interpretation revolves on the question as to the spiritual condition of the readers. Are they non-Christians who are weighing the matter of forsaking Judaism for Christianity? Are they Hebrew Christians who are tempted to forsake Christian-

ity for Judaism? Or are they Hebrew Christians who are
in danger of suffering from an arrested development in
their Christian experience? All these possibilities have
had their champions. Involved in one's position is the
question: Can a person be saved and then be lost again?
Also, can the soul be saved and the life be lost? Obviously
there are grave consequences involved in whatever attitude one adopts.

In our judgment it is quite clear that the author has
in mind those who have had a genuine experience of
grace (4:14-16; 6:1-3, 9-11f; 10:21-25; 12:1-2). Furthermore, there is ample evidence of an arrested development in their Christian experience (3:17 to 4:13; 5:12
to 6:6; 6:9-19; 10:35-39; 11:39-40; 12; 13). The entire tone
of the epistle implies their danger of falling short of
their ultimate destiny both in this age and in the age
to come (3:7-19). This danger is emphasized by the
Roman persecution which they are enduring (10:32-39;
12:4) and which is aggravated by their spiritual immaturity. In the particular passage at hand (2:1-4) it
seems that the author is thinking primarily of the fact
that his readers have become static in their Christian
experience. They have lost the first brilliance of their
new found life, and are in danger of failing to achieve
that for which Christ has laid hold on them.

Turning to the text, we find that the author's warning
to them begins with a reminder of the superior revelation
which they have in Christ. "Therefore," because God's
revelation in his Son is better, they ought to give to it
the more earnest heed—"lest at any time we should let
them slip" (2:1). Unhappily this translation has led
many to suppose that the author implies that they can
lose their salvation. The American Standard Version,
while giving the true meaning of the root word, falls
short when it reads "lest haply we drift away from them,"

implying that the Christian can drift away from or by the Christian truth. Neither of these seems to fit the context.

The word in question is *pararuōmen,* whose root meaning is to flow by or to drift by. Ignoring the danger of appearing technical, let us examine this word in the exact form that the author chose to use it. The verb form is the second aorist passive subjunctive, which means to have something happen to you. We find ourselves in agreement with the translation suggested by Dr. Edward A. McDowell—"lest perchance *we be drifted by,*" or *we be flowed by.* Says he: "You will note how I translated the last verb. It is the second aorist passive subjunctive, and the idea suggested is that the person is stationary and the things that were heard flow by him."

In short, the river of God's redemptive purpose as revealed in Christ Jesus flows on. These Christians have merely put their feet into the water at its edge. They are in it but barely so. The author's implied exhortation is for them to launch out into the main current of Christian growth and service as they fit themselves for their destined place in God's redemptive plan for all men. The river seems to say to them, "There is more!" While they splash idly in the shallows, the great current of the fuller Christian life passes them by.

2. *The Penalty for Neglect (2:2-4)*

The author hastens to remind his readers that this matter is no mere trifle. The greatness of their danger is illustrated from the Old Testament. It is impossible to understand Hebrews apart from the Old Testament passages which are a counterpart to the thoughts contained in it. "For if the word spoken by angels was stedfast, and every transgression and disobedience received a just recompence of reward," should they not all the more beware of their neglect of the revelation which is in Christ? Examples of this truth abound. "But the soul that doeth ought presumptuously, whether he be born in the land, or a stranger, the same reproacheth the Lord; and that soul shall be cut off from among his people" (Num. 15:30).

The context of this warning shows the penalty for presumptuous sin against the revelation through angels to be death by stoning. The offender was not lost from God, but by death he was cut off from among his people. He did not realize the blessed achievements prepared of the Lord for those who were faithful to the purpose of their calling.

On this factual basis the author implies the same experience for them. If our fathers could not without penalty ignore the partial revelation by angels, "how shall we escape, if we neglect so great salvation" which has come to us through the Son? It was first spoken by the Lord, then confirmed to us by those who heard him. Furthermore, God authenticated it by "signs and wonders, and with divers miracles, and gifts of the Holy Ghost, according to his own will" (2:3-4).

Turning again to the exhortation, we find that three words stand out: "neglect," "drift by," and "salvation." The first refers to their attitude toward the revelation. The second points to the result of their neglect. The third focuses attention upon that which is neglected.

"Salvation" is the key word here. It is a great salvation. "So" is a superlative which defies man's comprehension, as we see in the phrase "God so loved" (John 3:16). But *salvation* is the pivotal thought of the entire passage. What is the salvation whose neglect causes us to *be flowed by?* The word "which" may be enlarged into "which very salvation." The salvation in question is the very salvation which is the heart of God's revelation in his Son. What kind of salvation is it?

These Hebrew Christians faced the same peril which besets all Christians in every age. They regarded salvation simply as an initial experience apart from the continuing growth in grace, knowledge, and service of the Lord Jesus Christ (2 Peter 3:18). They needed to distinguish between *regeneration* and *salvation*. As we shall see later, the Israelites in Egypt were *redeemed (regenerated)* from death by the Lord through the blood of the paschal lamb; but they fell short of God's goal for them through their unbelief in the wilderness (Heb. 3:1 to 4:8). This does not mean that they were lost from God; in a sense they were cut off from the "rest" promised to them by the Lord. In other words, they received *redemption,* but they failed to achieve *salvation.*

Salvation, while it includes redemption, involves more. It goes beyond the initial experience to the full development of Christian character in grace, knowledge, and service. Thus salvation is instantaneous, continuing, and ultimate. The Hebrew Christians had experienced the instantaneous new birth, but they were not going on in growth unto the perfect man (Eph. 4:13). They were saved, "yet so as by fire." Their works are in danger of being destroyed (1 Cor. 3:13-15). For this reason they should give "the more earnest heed to the things which we have heard" (v. 1).

III. THE PURPOSE OF DIVINE REVELATION (2:5-18)

The danger of being flowed by because of their neglect of this great salvation is further emphasized as the author points out the purpose of God's revelation in a Son and which is not to be achieved through angels (v. 5). In this revelation God has a purpose, the purpose being to bring "many sons unto glory" (v. 10). Therefore, in being drifted by, not only do they lose their destiny, but they serve to thwart in their lives the very purpose of God.

1. The Dignity and Destiny of Man (2:5-8)

Man is ever ready to belittle his own dignity. With David he is content to say, "What is man, that thou art mindful of him? or the son of man [not Jesus, but man], that thou visitest him?" (v. 6; cf. Psalm 8:4). But the truth remains that God is mindful of man and has *visited* him. God has higher things in store for man than man realizes. "Thou [God] madest him a little [for a little while] lower than the angels; thou crownedst him with glory and honour, and didst set him over the works of thy hands: thou hast put all things [the universe] in subjection under his feet. For in that he put all in subjection under him, he left nothing that is not put under him" (vv. 7-8; cf. Psalm 8:5-6).

This is obviously a reference to God's original purpose in the creation of man, whose destiny is twofold. He is to "have dominion" over God's natural creation (Gen. 1:26), and he is to have fellowship or partnership (cf. *visiteth*) with God in the spiritual realm. In Eden he was told to have dominion over the earth and its creatures. This, however, was but a proving ground for greater things to come. In anticipation God crowned man with a glory and honor not given to any other of his created beings, including angels. To exercise this authority, man had to be free, free to make choices. It was in the exercise of this privilege that man lost his dignity and imperiled his spiritual destiny.

"But now we see not yet all things put under him" (v. 8). Despite the original dignity of man, our author points out that he has fallen far short of his destiny. When man sinned, he lost his partnership with God and his place of dominion over the natural creation. Henceforth, by the sweat of his brow and his brain he has slowly regained a degree of control over the forces of nature. But not even the marvelous material achievements of our present day approach the dominion once promised to man. His true destiny lies not in material mastery but in spiritual conquest. From Abraham onward we see that destiny developing as God *visited* with man to point out his original and abiding purpose in the redemption of the race. Man was to be blessed with material things only in order that he might be a blessing in spiritual matters (Gen. 12:2-3). Through the ages man has striven to excel in the realm of the material, but he has been derelict in his efforts to achieve his spiritual destiny.

Apart from the redemptive purpose of God in Christ, man is doomed never to receive again the dominion and partnership once promised. It is to this end that the author exhorts his readers to go on in their Christian experience. Man's hope in the beginning lay in the glory and honor with which he was crowned. Being spiritual, his destiny lies in that direction. Thus far man within himself has failed. His destiny resides within another.

2. The Role of the Son of Man (2:9-16)

"But we see Jesus." Here is the factor which makes the difference. Through the revelation of prophets and angels man fell short of God's goal. It was then that God stepped from eternity into time. Thus the reference is to the incarnation. If God was to bring "many sons unto glory," it must be not by the power of man but through the power of God. Jesus, then, is God's last word to man and man's last hope toward God.

We see, therefore, that the incarnation was a necessity. Through it, "for a little while" [author's translation], Jesus himself was made "lower than the angels" (v. 9), passing by the nature of angels, through whom no one was to be redeemed, to take on himself the seed of Abraham through whom God's purpose in redemption was to run. He entered fully into the experience of man. Sin was the interloper which spoiled the destiny of man. And since the wages of sin is death, God himself in the person of his Son paid the full price for sin when he tasted "death for [in the place of] every man" (v. 9), that he might redeem man in his entirety. Because of this, God has crowned Jesus with glory and honor (v. 9; cf. Phil. 2:9-11), that he might achieve for man that glory and honor which man could not achieve for himself.

Man could be perfected only through a perfect Saviour. The Creator and Sustainer of the universe could be made perfect only through sufferings (v. 10). As *Creator* and *Sustainer* of the universe he exercised *dominion* over the material order. But it was only through his suffering death for sin that he could enter into the *partnership of* redemption. This was the "glory and honour" with which he was crowned (cf. Rev. 5:12). Thus, not in his mastery of nature does man recover the "glory and honour" for which he is destined. It is only as he fulfils his destiny of partnership with Christ in world redemption. Achieving this, man, who for a little while was made lower than the angels, will with Christ reign over angels and over all of God's creation in "the world to come" (2:5). In this sense for Jesus to be made *perfect* refers not to freedom from fault, but rather to fitness for a given task. In his humanity Jesus entered into the full experience of man, apart from sin, in order to be identified with man in his struggle to achieve the destiny for which God had made him (vv. 14-15). One can know life only by living it (v. 16). There is no moral imperfection in Jesus, but he became man in order to be "a sympathizing and effective leader in the work of salvation" (Robertson).

Thus Jesus became one with man. The "Sanctifier"

and the "sanctified" are brethren (v. 11). Together they praise God (v. 12); together they must have faith in God (v. 13). Together they must achieve their destiny, the one as a Son of God, the others as sons of God.

3. The Goal of Man Through the Son of Man (2:17-18)

The crux of the whole matter is at this point. "Wherefore" encompasses the whole of the author's argument up to this juncture. We repeat, the purpose of God's revelation which was climaxed in the humiliation and death of his Son was to bring "many sons unto glory," to enable them to achieve their destiny, a destiny which they failed to achieve through the revelation which came by men and angels. Their destiny lay not in being angels by and by, as we sometimes sing. Instead, it lay in their becoming true sons of Abraham as they became partners with Jesus in using their material mastery for spiritual ends. Before man could do this, he had to be redeemed from sin. This redemption had been accomplished by the revelation through a Son who was "made like unto his brethren" (v. 17) in order that his brethren might be made like unto him.

It is significant that for the first time, in verse 17, the author introduces the picture of Jesus as our "merciful and faithful high priest." The office of the high priest included two responsibilities, sacrifice and intercession. In the one he worked for the redemption of man; in the other he ministered to the end that man might be a fit subject to enter into fellowship with God in worship and service. The author has reminded the Hebrew Christians that Jesus has always identified himself with them for their redemption or reconciliation (v. 17). He now suggests that he has further identified himself with them in his finished sacrifice and in his intercession for their complete salvation (v. 18).

The burden of their problem was the temptation to lose their destiny through the neglect of their continuing growth in the Christian calling. Because of this, they face the danger of being flowed by. But in their temptation there is help at hand. As their High Priest, Jesus, having endured the trials of human living, is one who can be touched with their infirmities (4:15). He knows the temptation to stop short of one's destiny. Repeatedly he had to grapple with the urge to stop short of the cross. Because of this he is able "to succour them that are tempted" (v. 18). The word "succour" means to run at a cry or call for help. Thus they need not struggle with their temptation alone. Instead they should call for help, and their High Priest will run to their aid. The one who redeemed them can enable them to go on to a full salvation. Therefore they should not be content to let life flow by but should go on in their development until they achieve that for which they are destined.

For Review and Further Study

1. What are the three elements in revelation? Who is the source of revelation? Name some of the human instruments of revelation. What does the author mean by "divers manners" and "at sundry times"? Who is the instrument of God's final revelation?

2. Was the Epistle to the Hebrews written to saved or unsaved people? Give the true meaning of the words "let them slip." What are the three elements involved in salvation?

3. What is the dignity of man? What is his destiny? How does Jesus help man in achieving his destiny?

4. What is man's duty in the light of God's better revelation?

3

THE WARNING
FROM HISTORY

[3:1 to 4:13]

At this point the purpose of the author becomes quite clear. Most certainly he is writing with genuine Christians in mind, for he refers to them as "holy brethren." They are the "sanctified" whom the "Sanctifier" is happy to call "brethren" (2:11). Furthermore, they are "partakers of [partners in] the heavenly calling" (3:1). They have been called from heaven and to heaven. This *upward* calling relates itself to the exhortation not to be flowed by. In his previous argument the author has established the fact that through the better revelation in a Son they have been redeemed. More clearly now, and with greater emphasis, he urges them to go on unto the full purpose of God's revelation. In so doing he cites the history of Israel's failure as a warning to them.

The basis of his continued appeal is that just as Christianity has a better revelation in Jesus over that which came through the prophets and the angels, so does it have a better ministry through Jesus than through Moses. His argument is stronger here as may be seen in the fact that the Jews regarded Moses as being the first and greatest prophet. Also they held him in greater esteem than they held the angels. Rabbi Jose ben Chalafta, in the second century, echoed this attitude when, in commenting on Numbers 12:7, he said, "God calls Moses 'faithful

in all his house,' and thereby he ranked higher than the
ministering angels themselves."

I. THE PERSON FOR THE MINISTRY (3:1-6)

1. *He Is Both an Apostle, a High Priest, and a Saviour (vv. 1-2)*

The beginning of Judaism as a historical religion may
be said to date from the event when God spoke to Moses
in Midian saying, "Come now therefore, and *I will send
thee* [author's italics] unto Pharaoh, that thou mayest
bring forth my people the children of Israel out of Egypt"
(Ex. 3:10). From this humble origin we have the elaborate system of laws (Moses) and sacrifices (Aaron) which
comprise the basic elements of the Judaism out of which
the Hebrew Christians had come.

In his words "I will send thee" God, in effect, is declaring Moses to be his *apostle* to the Israelites, that he
might be an instrument in God's hand for their redemption and for preparation in turn for their own redemptive ministry. *Beyond redemption (used in the Christian
sense of the initial experience of regeneration) from
Egypt he was to lead the Israelites through the wilderness
into the Promised Land.* Although "Moses was faithful
in all his [God's] house" (v. 2), it would be evident to
the readers of the epistle that he failed to perform completely the ministry which was entrusted to him. By
God's power he led Israel in her redemption from bondage, but failed to carry them forward to their ultimate
destiny. In this the author offers no criticism of Moses,
but by subtle intimation reminds his readers that Moses'
ministry, while incomplete, was successful under the
leadership of Joshua (Hebrew for "Jesus"), the saviour of
the Old Testament.

In the light of the incomplete ministry of Moses in
their former profession, the author urges the Hebrew

Christians to "consider the Apostle and High Priest of *our profession* [author's italics], Christ Jesus" (v. 1). In the original the text simply uses "Jesus," the human name of our incarnate Lord. Thus he focuses their attention again upon the earthly ministry of "a Son." His reference to Jesus as our High Priest, previously mentioned, is taken up later. The emphasis at this time is upon the comparison of the ministry of the apostle Moses and the Apostle Jesus. Only here in the New Testament is Jesus called an Apostle, although there are many references to him as having been sent from God. As God sent Moses to redeem and lead the Israelites to the realization of God's purpose for them, so did he send Jesus to redeem and lead the new Israel into the full experience of God's plan for them. Likewise, in contrast to the apostle Moses (redeemer) whose ministry was completed only through the aid of Aaron (priest) and Joshua (saviour), our Apostle Jesus is Redeemer, Priest, and Saviour, who is able to accomplish that for which God sent him. Thus "our profession" has a greater Apostle than that of the old profession out of which the Hebrew Christians came.

2. *He Is the Builder of God's House (vv. 3-4)*

The superior ministry of Jesus as our Apostle is further emphasized as the author changes the figure from that of Apostle to that of Builder. Already he has referred to God's house (v. 2), a term used to indicate the people of God. In his ministry Moses was not charged with the responsibility of building up the house of God, for it was already in existence (11:2, 25). Moses himself was a part of that house, and, as such, even though he was faithful in the house of God, he was not its builder.

On the other hand, Jesus, our Apostle, is the builder of the house of God. He founded it of old, and he builds it out of those like Moses who through faith are "built up a spiritual house ... " (1 Peter 2:5). Since the builder is greater than the house, so is Jesus greater than Moses. "For this man was counted worthy of more glory than Moses, inasmuch as he who hath builded the house hath more honour than the house" (v. 3). Just as Moses who built the tabernacle was greater than the tabernacle, even so Jesus, infinitely so, is greater than Moses. The truth is so obvious that the author refuses to elaborate upon it other than to use it as an occasion to ascribe deity to Jesus (v. 4).

3. He Is a Son over the Servant (vv. 5-6)

Furthermore, the superior ministry of Jesus over that of Moses is seen in the fact that the latter is a servant in God's house, while the former is a Son over the house—his own house—and over Moses (v. 6). Moses was a faithful servant, but his ministry was but a witness to that which was to come (v. 5). This witness was fulfilled in Jesus, the Lord of the house. As a servant Moses was under authority; as a Son Jesus possessed authority. As a servant Moses ministered in God's house; as a Son Jesus ministered to his house. Hence the ministry of Jesus is better than that of Moses.

II. THE PERSONS OF THE MINISTRY (3:7-19)

Both the ministry of Moses and of Jesus was directed toward persons. In the former these persons were the Israelites; in the latter they were the Hebrew Christians and others like them who are redeemed by Jesus. Using the former as an example, the author proceeds to issue another warning to the latter, as he infers that while they are the objects of the ministry of Jesus, they also have a ministry to perform for him. To this end he both warns and exhorts them. In his first exhortation the writer indicated that the danger of failure on the part of the Hebrew Christians was due to their *neglect* of this great salvation. Here the author is dealing with the more positive attitude of *refusal* to go on in their Christian calling unto its intended goal. In so doing he points out the cause of the failure of the ministry of Moses—the rebellion of the people who had been redeemed.

1. *The Example of Israel (vv. 7-11)*

This entire section is a quotation of Psalm 95:7-11 in which the psalmist warns against a refusal to bow down and worship God. Some see in this passage a reference to the incident at Rephidim (Ex. 17:1-7) when the Israelites murmured against Moses because they had no water. However, the context in Hebrews seems to refer the quotation to the rebellion of Israel at Kadesh-barnea (Num. 13f.). This identification is important, for upon it turns the interpretation of much of the Epistle to the Hebrews. We must know exactly what was in the mind of the author.

Let it be remembered that the Israelites had been redeemed from bondage and death in Egypt by their faith in the blood of the paschal lamb (Ex. 12). Following this redemption they were to go through the trials of the wilderness into the land of Canaan where they should fulfil their destiny as "a kingdom of priests, and an holy nation" (Ex. 19:6). From this vantage point in the ancient world they were to become the priests of God in his plan of redemption for the whole human race. Two years later they are at the borders of the land of promise. From the report of ten of the spies it is apparent that they still have a struggle before them if they are to enter in. At this thought the people rebel, declaring that they would rather have died in Egypt or in the wilderness. It is even suggested that they select another "captain" in

the place of Moses that they might return to Egypt.
Turning deaf ears to the pleas of Moses, Aaron, Joshua,
and Caleb, the people are on the verge of stoning them
to death. Note that this final rebellion was the climax
of many sins of the past. Thus it is called by the psalmist
and by our author "the provocation."

At that crucial moment "the glory of the Lord appeared," and the Lord said to Moses, "How long will this
people provoke (cf. Heb. 3:8) me? and how long will it
be ere they believe (cf. Heb. 3:12, 18f.) me? . . . I will
smite them with the pestilence, and disinherit them"
(Num. 14:11f.) *Note that while God threatens to destroy
the nation, he says nothing about the possibility of their
returning to the bondage of Egypt.*

But for the prayer of Moses, the apostle and minister
of God now turned priest, the sentence of God would
have been carried out. They would have perished and
would have been disinherited, no longer being a people
of God. In his prayer Moses reminded God that his very
name was at stake among the pagan peoples whom God
wanted to redeem. "Now if thou shalt kill all this people
as one man, then the nations which have heard the fame
of thee will speak, saying, Because the Lord was not able
to bring this people into the land which he sware unto
them, therefore he hath slain them in the wilderness"
(Num. 14:15f.). Moses further reminds God that his
greater power is shown not in might but in mercy. Therefore he pleads for God to forgive his people, which God
does, saying, "I have pardoned according to thy word"
(v. 20). They are still the people of God. But because of
their sin of provocation that generation shall die natural
deaths in the wilderness, not entering the Promised Land
where they were to have been used of God in world
redemption. Instead, he reminds them of the "altering
of my purpose" (marginal reading, v. 34) by which Joshua

and Caleb shall lead their children to the fulfilment of the purpose which God had desired for them. The marginal reading in the American Standard Version is "the revoking of my purpose." This would imply their loss of the covenant relation. They did not defeat the ultimate purpose of God, but as a generation they lost the privilege of sharing in it.

The point of this illustration is clear. Israel, through the ministry of Moses, had been redeemed from the bondage of Egypt. While, in the face of trial, they refuse to go on to the achievement of their divine destiny, it is impossible for them to return to their former state. Although *they* contemplate doing just that, the decision is not theirs to make. They are in the hands of the God who redeemed them (cf. John 10:28). However, because they refused to believe, they did lose the privilege of being used of God in his redemptive plan for all nations. We repeat, they did not defeat that purpose, but they did delay it for a generation. Because of this, God swore that they should not enter into his *rest* (v. 11).

2. *The Example Applied to Hebrew Christians (vv. 12-15)*

These Hebrew Christians are in danger of the same sad experience. Their redemption is genuine and complete. However, they face the decision of either going on to a full salvation or of refusing to do so, full salvation in their case meaning redemption, Christian growth, and redemptive service. The trial of persecution is causing them to *provoke* God. Perhaps because of a superficial experience, some have turned back to the comparative safety of Judaism. Others, with a genuine experience of grace, are contemplating such, but the author infers from the experience of Israel that they cannot do so. The danger of these Hebrew Christians is to lose the blessing of full part-

nership with God in his plan of redemption for the whole
world. They shall not defeat that plan, but may delay it.
Because of this, God will simply pass them by, in the
altering of his purpose, while others shall go on to a full
realization of God's purpose for them.

That this is the case may be seen as we examine this
exhortation (vv. 12-15). "Take heed" serves to connect
it with the preceding illustration. In this warning two
words stand out: "unbelief" (*apistias*) and "departing
from" (*apostēnai*). In order to understand the warning
we must render these words, apart from the English words
used to translate them, in their original form and in
their own thought context.

Apistias (unbelief) is an obvious reference to Jehovah's
question, "How long . . . ere they believe me?" (Num.
14:11). The point is not that the Israelites did not believe
in God's power to redeem them from Egypt. They could
not doubt that, for it had already occurred. That was no
longer a matter of faith but of fact. In short, they did
not disbelieve God; they simply had not believed that
he could lead them into Canaan. Despite the miracles
which he had already shown them in the past, the brilliance of their former experiences in faith had so faded
that they did not believe him for their future trials and
ultimate victory. The point here is not a past faith dis-
avowed, but a future faith not yet expressed.

In this light let us examine the word *apistias*. Its root
comes from a verb meaning *I believe* or *I trust*. The
substantive form means faith or belief. In Greek the
alpha privative placed before a word gives to the word
its opposite meaning. Here, then, the author uses *pistias*
(faith) with the alpha privative which gives us *apistias* or
no faith. In other words, it means no faith at all. Thus our
author cites the Israelites' failure to believe in God's
power for future conquests as a warning that they should

beware lest they have no faith in God for their endurance through the trial of persecution into a full realization of his will for them.

The word *apostēnai* is fraught with many dangers. It is an infinitive taken from the Greek verb which means *to stand off from,* or *to step aside from.* It sometimes meant *to excite to revolt* (Acts 5:37). It is used in this sense in the Septuagint version of Ezekiel 20:8. Much help in determining the exact meaning of a Greek word is derived from the papyri. This is a vast group of written items such as social, legal, and economic records which show the usage of words in the everyday life of the people of New Testament times. In the papyri *apostatēs* is used to refer to *rebels.*

Another derivative from this root verb found in the papyri is *apostasion* which is used in the sense of renouncing a contract. This same word is used in the papyri and in the New Testament (Matt. 19:7) in the sense of a divorcement from marriage. Thayer's Lexicon cites the use of *apostēnai* in Hebrews 3:12 as *to fall away* in the sense of *becoming faithless.* From this same verb we get the word *apostasia* which we translate *apostasy.* The usual and modern meaning of apostasy is the act of giving up what one has professed, believed, or followed, as religious or political apostasy. In this sense to apostatize from the living God would mean to turn one's back upon him, suggesting the loss of redemption. Naturally this meaning may be read into our text. However, it must be interpreted not as a proof text but as a part of the entire body of the New Testament. If that be done, we shall find that the burden of proof will lie upon those who insist upon the possibility of one who has been genuinely saved ever being lost from God. The author of the epistle himself assumes that such is not the case (6:9ff.).

To what, then, does the word *apostēnai* refer? Keeping

in mind the illustration of Israel in the light of which we
are compelled to interpret verse 12, what do we find?
Israel, redeemed from bondage, came right up to the
borders of Canaan, their intended destination from
which they were to render a specific service for God.
Because they allowed the peril of going on to dim their
memories as to God's mighty works for them in the past,
they refused to have faith that he could enable them to
triumph. Therefore they refused to go into Canaan. They
revolted against God's leadership in fulfilling their divine destiny (cf. Num. 14:9). When God, figuratively
speaking, stepped before them to lead them, they *stood
off from* him, they *stepped aside from* the living God.
They became faithless as to God's power to see them
through. In short, they renounced their covenant relationship in which they had agreed to be "a kingdom of
priests, and an holy nation" in God's redemptive plan.
For this they did not return to Egypt, even though *they*
considered the possibility. They simply perished in the
wilderness without realizing that better thing which God
had prepared for them. *There would appear here to be
no evidence of apostasy in the usual sense of the word.*

This very thing which the Israelites did, the Hebrew
Christians are in danger of doing. They have made the
start toward God's *rest* in that they have been redeemed,
a redemption which our author assumes to have been
genuine. However, the perils of persecution have
dimmed the brilliance of that experience, causing them
to be in danger of having no faith in their Redeemer to
lead them on to the full salvation for which they are
destined. As the "author and finisher" (12:2) of their
faith goes before them to lead them on, they are tempted
to *stand off from him,* to rebel against him, to re-
nounce their contract with the living God. Although,
like Israel they may be considering going back into their

unregenerate state (Judaism), they are unable to do so.

At this point we see the meaning of the words "the Apostle and High Priest ... even Jesus" (v. 1). With the wrath of God poised over them for their destruction and disinheritance, their Apostle becomes their High Priest to intercede for them. The very name and power of God in Christ is at stake. On their own merit they deserve to be lost, as they never deserved to be redeemed. But they are hidden with Christ in God (Col. 3:3). As such it is impossible for them ever to be lost from God. They are his, and at the plea of their High Priest the power of God is tempered in mercy, as God says, "I have pardoned according to thy [Christ's] word" (Num. 14:20). Nevertheless, because of their sin of standing off from Jesus, if they commit it, they shall not achieve the destiny which God has promised for them (Num. 14:23). The picture is the same throughout the epistle. They are not to *neglect* their salvation or *stand off from* their Saviour lest they *be flowed by*. As in *Numbers 13ff. so here there would appear to be no evidence of apostasy in the sense of losing their redemption.*

Such a position seems to make clear the author's meaning when he says, "But exhort one another daily, ... lest any of you be hardened through the deceitfulness of sin. For we are made partakers of Christ, if we hold the beginning of our confidence stedfast unto the end" (vv. 13-14). The sin referred to is *standing off from* God in failing to go on unto their intended destiny. The phrase "partakers of Christ" refers not to their initial experience of redemption. The original may more aptly be translated "partners with Christ." The Greek word is *metochoi*. It is used many times in the papyri in the sense of sharer or partner. It occurs both in the sense of associates in business and as joint owners of a business. The word is used only six times in the New Testament, once in Luke 5:7 and five times in Hebrews (1:9; 3:1; 3:14; 6:4; 12:8).

In Luke the occasion is that of the miraculous draught of fishes, where it has the same translation as we have noted in the papyri: "And they beckoned unto their partners . . . that they should come and help them." This same sense more fittingly gives the meaning of the word in all its uses in Hebrews. Thus in 1:9 Jesus is anointed with oil above his *partners*. In 3:1 the holy brethren are *partners* in the heavenly calling. In 6:4 they are *partners* with the Holy Spirit in God's redemptive purpose. In 12:8 they are *partners* in enduring chastisement. In 3:14 they are *partners* with Christ (cf. A. T. Robertson, *Word Pictures in the New Testament,* Baptist Sunday School Board, 1932, *in loco*) in the task of world redemption. But they can be partners with him only if they hold fast their earlier confidence that God in Christ is able to carry them through to their full spiritual experience. The author's use of the third conditional sentence implies that while it is not an accomplished fact, he believes that it will be.

3. *The Example Emphasized (vv. 16-19)*

Nevertheless, the author once more stresses his warning and adds an exhortation. Be sure that you do not harden your hearts to provoke God by standing off from him. If so, like those whose carcasses fell in the wilderness short of their intended destiny, so will you fail in God's purpose for you. Those who fell did so not because of Moses' unfaithfulness but because of their own lack of faith in God's power to lead them on (v. 19). Likewise, the Hebrew Christians will fail, if they do, not because of the unfaithfulness of their Apostle, Jesus, but by their own lack of faith in his power to sustain them in their present persecution and to lead them on to fulfil their destiny. To do so will not defeat the redemptive purpose of God for all men; it will only deprive them of the blessing of having a part in its realization.

III. THE PERFORMANCE OF THE MINISTRY (4:1-13)

1. *The Promise of a "Rest" (vv. 1, 4, 7, 8-9)*

The author now turns to a more detailed consideration of the goal of the ministry of Jesus. Moses' ministry had been incomplete because of the failure of the people to whom he ministered. The Hebrew Christians are exhorted not to "come short" (v. 1) by their failure, even though their "Apostle and High Priest" is well able to carry them through to their destiny. Their promised destiny the author refers to as God's "rest" (v. 1; cf. 3:11). This word is used to translate a Greek word which means to give rest. It is found in the Septuagint, but is used in the New Testament only in Acts 7:49 and in Hebrews 3:11 to 4:11. This section is a continuation of the author's treatment of Psalm 95, and should be considered in the light of our previous discussion.

To establish his meaning of the word "rest" the author uses it in three connections. His first reference is to the *rest* of God at the completion of his creative work (v. 4). His second reference is to the *rest* promised to the children of Israel upon their arrival in the land of Canaan (v. 5). That this rest was not the one which the author has in mind is seen in the fact that David promised yet another *rest*. "For if Jesus [Joshua] had given them rest, then would he not afterward have spoken of another day. There remaineth therefore a rest to the people of God" (v. 8-9). Thus the third reference to *rest* pertains to the experience for which the Hebrew Christians are destined under the leadership of Jesus, the Joshua (synonymous names in Greek and Hebrew) or Saviour of the better revelation.

The usual interpretation of the word "rest" as used in Hebrews is that it refers to heaven (cf. Acts 7:49). To this we partly agree. The author assumes that his readers are genuine Christians, and despite their continued sin of standing off from God with regard to their spiritual destiny, they are destined in Christ to arrive in heaven. However, if our thesis be a correct one, there is more involved. Here once more we have a reference to the Christian's spiritual mission. May we suggest that in the use of the word "rest" we have a sample of the influence which the allegorical method of interpretation so prevalent in Alexandria has upon our author, his readers, and his message (cf. Gal. 4:22-26). Remotely he has in mind the heavenly rest, but more immediately he is concerned with the Christian's Canaan or sabbath rest, which has to do with God's redemptive purpose through his people.

We have seen that the author has in mind the "provocation" at Kadesh-barnea. There the Israelites were not prevented from entering their rest because of their repeated sins between Egypt (redemption) and Kadesh-barnea. The "sin of provocation" was the climax of all of those in their refusal to enter into the land of their destiny, a destiny which was identified with their becoming instruments of God in world redemption. In Canaan they were not to cease from work; their work would just begin. Their *rest* was to be relief from the struggle to attain the land of their destiny.

This same truth emerges when we examine God's *rest* at the end of his creative work. Certainly God at that point did not cease from all activity. For this assertion we have no less authority than Jesus himself. "My Father worketh hitherto, and I work" (John 5:17). For the very work which Jesus did he was accused of breaking the sabbath rest. Therefore, after God had achieved his sabbath rest, he continued to work. Obviously he worked in the sustaining of his creation, as did Jesus. But the heart of the meaning is to be found elsewhere.

Immediately upon the finish of his work in creation, God began his work of redemption (Gen. 3:15). He was working at it in his charge to Abraham (Gen. 12), in the redemption of Israel from Egypt, and he was seeking to perform it through the promised *rest* of Israel in Canaan. It was this work of the Father which Jesus was doing in John 5 and in all his incarnate experience. It was this same work which God was seeking to do through the Hebrew Christians whom he had already redeemed from bondage and death.

In this light, therefore, let us look once again at the "rest to the people of God" (v. 9). The author changes his word here to denote *rest*. In his other references he has employed a Greek word, whose root idea is to give rest. In verse 9 he uses a word not found elsewhere in Greek literature, except for a doubtful reference in Plutarch (Robertson). Apparently he coins a word to express his exact idea. The word is *sabbatismos,* derived from the verb which means to keep the sabbath (Ex. 16:30). If we remember that God is mentioned as resting "the seventh day from all his works" (v. 4), the author's idea begins to appear. The seventh day was the Jewish sabbath which commemorated God's *rest* after creation. We have seen, however, that on that sabbath, which is regarded as still going on, God did not cease to work. He merely changed his activity from that of creation to redemption.

Therefore the Hebrew Christians are not urged to achieve a *katapausis* but a *sabbatismos,* or a sabbath kind of rest. In it they shall rest from their works as God did from his (v. 10). But it will not be a cessation of activity. Their rest will be from the struggle to attain their destiny

in the face of persecution, as God's rest was an end to his
work in creation. (Of course, we are not to regard God's
creative work as one of physical struggle or effort.) As
God changed his activity from that of creation to redemption, so are the Hebrew Christians in their *sabbatismos* to change their work from that of a struggle to
achieve their goal of Christian character into that of becoming partners (3:14) with Christ in redemptive service.

2. *The Peril of God's People (vv. 1-3)*

Running through this entire section is the repeated
note of warning lest the Hebrew Christians "come short"
of this worthy goal (v. 1). The same glad tidings were
preached to the Israelites, but they did not profit by them
because of their lack of faith in God. The reference here
is not simply to a gospel of redemption, but to the fuller
gospel of realizing their full goal of Christian character
and service.

But those who have faith in God's power to perform
his will shall "enter into rest" (v. 3). The work of redemption was "finished from the foundation of the
world" (v. 3; cf. Rev. 13:8), but their work in God's redemptive plan waits upon their faith in the eternal God
to perform it.

3. *The Need for Perseverance (vv. 11-13)*

Here the author calls for an immediate consecration
of all their faculties to God. "Let us labour [hasten, or
be eager and alert] therefore to enter into that rest" (v.
11). The best defense against the danger of obstinate disobedience is a positive acceptance of God's full will for
them. The word "unbelief" (v. 11) is a mistranslation of
a Greek word meaning disobedience, obstinacy, rebellion
against orders, and, particularly in the New Testament,

obstinate opposition to the divine will (cf. Rom. 11:30, 32; Heb. 4:6).

To reach this state of dedication requires constant self-examination as to their innermost attitudes and purposes (vv.12-13). Although they may fool others, or even themselves, they cannot hide them from God. For the word [*logos,* which could be a veiled reference to Jesus] of God is "living" (cf. 3:12), and "energetic," [author's translation] and "sharper" than any two-edged sword. It is "piercing" to the point of dividing the soul and spirit, the joints and marrow, and even to discerning the thoughts and intents of the heart. Thus God through his Word is a theologian who understands our spiritual needs; a surgeon who can aid in our physical needs; a psychologist who can analyze and direct the very thoughts and intents of our hearts.

Therefore none can hide from God, for his microscope can reveal the smallest microbe of doubt or disobedience. Body and soul are naked before him. Our inmost secrets are laid open (v. 13) before him. The word used here is one which means to bend back the neck as the surgeon does for an operation. Thus, as the inner organs of our bodies are laid open before the eyes of the surgeon, so are the inmost facts of our hearts revealed before "the eyes of him [God] with whom we have to do" (v. 13). Literally translated this last phrase reads "with whom the matter or account [*logos*] for us is" (Robertson). Here we see a play on the word *logos.* God through his *logos* (word) has to do with our *logos* (account). God's *logos* is not only sharp and revealing to lay bare before God our failures; it is also living and active in enabling us to overcome our temptation to fail, that we might go on to the achievement of God's goal for us. In the accomplishment of this work Jesus will fulfil his ministry and we shall begin ours.

For Review and Further Study

1. What is the significance of Jesus being our Apostle, High Priest, and Saviour? In what ways is Jesus superior to Moses?

2. Read Numbers 13-14. What is meant by "the provocation"? Give the true meaning of "unbelief" and "falling away." What is the significance of the phrase "partakers of Christ"?

3. Give the three senses in which the author uses the word "rest." In what sense is the "rest" which is offered the Christian in this life like a sabbath rest?

4

THE BASIS OF HOPE

[4:14 to 7:28]

THE AUTHOR of Hebrews presents the priesthood of Jesus as the basis of the hope of God's people in their Christian calling. Already he has alluded to the fact (1:3; 2:17f.; 3:1). Now he proposes to discuss it at length (4:14 to 12:3), showing in every respect that Christianity has a better priesthood than Judaism. In the Old Testament the priest ministered to a redeemed people but was unable to bring them to the destiny God intended for them.

It is in this light that we must understand the author's presentation of Jesus as the High Priest of the new revelation. He, too, ministers to a redeemed people who have a destiny before them. They are in danger of falling short of it, and for that reason the author urges upon them the truth that they are not alone in their struggle for achievement. They have been redeemed by the Apostle of their profession; now they may be kept by the High Priest of that same profession (3:1).

I. THE FACT OF HIS PRIESTHOOD DECLARED (4:14 to 5:11)

1. *He Is Our Great High Priest (vv. 14-16)*

The author identifies him as "Jesus the Son of God" (v. 14). The first title refers to his humanity; the second speaks of his deity. He is no longer *a* Son of God but *the* Son of God. He, therefore, is a definite person whom they can identify in their history. He is the source of their re-

demption, a redemption which they received through
the death, burial, and resurrection of the incarnate Son
of God. So much they will readily admit. However, this
is past history, even though it is in the recent past. Like
the Israelites before Mount Sinai they can say, "As for
this Jesus, we know not what has become of him. His
work of redemption is all right for the past, but what
about our present predicament?"

It is to this inferred question that the author now
turns. This same Jesus, he tells them, is still ministering
to them in their present trial. He has "passed into the
heavens," into the very presence of God, to enable them
to "hold fast our profession" (v. 14). Furthermore, since
he is the same Jesus who took upon himself the "weaknesses" of men, he is able to understand their present
trial and to enable them to triumph over it (v. 15). "Let
us therefore come boldly unto the throne of grace, that
we may obtain mercy [forgiveness for our sin of waver-
ing], and find grace to help in time of need" (v. 16).

Volumes are contained in these brief words. What is
meant by "infirmities"? How may we interpret the temptations of Jesus? The word "infirmities" may best be
translated *weaknesses*. Here the author doubtless refers
to our Lord's identification with us in human flesh. The
human mind cannot fathom the depths of this mystery.
In his weakness Jesus was certainly no less God than
when he was in the bosom of the Father. But somehow he
carried in his glorious person the nature of man, apart
from its sinful aspects. We must recognize, then, that
weakness refers not to moral defection but to the physical
limits of human flesh such as hunger, thirst, weariness,
and the like. Because of these self-assumed weaknesses
Jesus was subjected to temptation, and Satan did his
utmost in all these realms to seduce the Son of God.

That Jesus was tempted we may be sure. The gospel

record is full of that fact. The question is as to what extent his temptations ran and to what degree were they real. To say that they were not real is to accuse Jesus of sham, which is repulsive to us all. To say that he could not sin is to beg the question. Our author plainly says that he was tempted at all points or according to all things such as man experiences temptation. In reverence we draw back from the logical conclusion; but it is there nevertheless, or else words have no meaning. Of course, we agree with Dr. A. T. Robertson that Jesus possessed no latent sin to be stirred by temptation, and with Dr. James Moffatt that there were some temptations which were impossible to him for they arise out of sins previously committed. But it was necessary that Jesus be tempted or tested that through the same he might be able to sympathize (v. 15) with man in his trials.

The glorious conclusion of the whole matter is stated in the fact that Jesus was tempted "yet without sin" or apart from sin. But the question immediately arises: If Jesus stopped short of personal sin, how can he *sympathize* with us in our temptations? We answer this question with another question. Who knows the full force of temptation, the man who gives in to it at an early stage before it has done its worst, or the man who endures to the end and triumphs over it? The answer is quite evident. Thus Jesus can fully sympathize with us more than we can sympathize with ourselves, for he knows the full agony of temptation.

The temptation of immediate concern to our author is that which results in disobedience to the will of God with regard to a predetermined destiny. This was the one which was besetting (12:1) the Hebrew Christians. Of interest is the fact that this is the only temptation of Jesus which is specifically treated in the Gospels, and it was repeated many times. Therefore their High Priest

was tempted in all things, as they were, to turn his back
upon God's will for his life—apart from actually sub-
mitting to it. Thus he knows what it is to be tempted
to think of his own safety without regard to God's will
for his life (Matt. 4:3). He is aware of the inducements
to alter the purpose of God to his own ends (Matt. 4:6;
John 6:15). He can understand the sinister lure of taking
the easy way out of the gory road over which he is destined
to travel (Matt. 4:8f.; 27:40). All these temptations he
had in common with these Hebrew Christians. But in
every one of them "he stedfastly set his face to go to
Jerusalem" (Luke 9:51), knowing that at the end of
that road lay shame, suffering, death—and the fulfilment
of God's purpose for him. As the result of his own
experience, therefore, "he is able to succour [run to their
cry for help] them that are tempted" (2:18) to turn their
backs upon the will of God; and to give "grace to help
in [the] time" of their specific need (4:16). In that assurance they are to stand fast in the face of their present
persecution.

2. *He Meets the Qualifications for High Priesthood* (5:1-9)

There were two essential qualifications necessary for
one to occupy the office of high priest. He must be taken
from among men to minister to men (v. 1), and he must
be appointed of God (v. 4). Such was necessary that the
high priest, having been appointed of God, might "bear
gently" (Robertson) with the ignorant and the erring
(v. 2), offering both gifts and sacrifices to God for his
own sins (except in the case of Jesus), as well as for the
sins of others.

Having established the fact of Jesus' divine appointment (vv. 5-6), the author points out that Jesus was
qualified to *bear gently* with those who were being

tempted (v. 7). It is significant that he selects the Geth-
semane experience of Jesus which marked Satan's last
attempt that side of the cross to turn Jesus back from
the role of his eternal destiny. Here Jesus "in the days
of his flesh, . . . offered up prayers and supplications with
strong crying and tears unto him that was able to save
him from death" (v. 7). We see here the intensity of the
temptation which Jesus had to bear.

The word "death" involves more than the mere act of
dying. Jesus was not afraid of death in that sense. Martyrs
by the thousands have gladly faced death in his name,
and Jesus was no less courageous than they. That from
which Jesus sought deliverance was that which his death
involved, namely, that in order to be the Redeemer he
had to identify himself completely with man's sin. "For
he hath made him to be sin for us, who knew no sin;
that we might be made the righteousness of God in him"
(2 Cor. 5:21). Having resisted the full force of temptation apart from sin, still he must become the very
essence of sin. This was necessary if he was to fulfil his
destiny.

It is of interest to note that while because of his
"godly fear" (Robertson) God heard him, yet he did not
permit him to turn back. Instead, through the ministry
of angels (1:14), God gave to him grace to endure the
suffering that in doing so he might be made *perfect*. The
root meaning of that word is not freedom from fault,
for Jesus needed no such. Rather it refers to fitness for
a given task. As such, therefore, Jesus was made complete
for his intended role as "the author [Pioneer] of eternal
salvation unto all them that obey him" (v. 9). Keeping
in mind the threefold nature of salvation as set forth in
chapter 2, we see that Jesus is the Pioneer or Beginner
of their salvation in that he has redeemed them. This
he accomplished through his obedience to God (v. 8).

The completion of the process of their salvation is dependent upon their obedience to him. It is in this realm that his role of High Priest is significant.

3. *He Has a Greater High Priesthood (vv. 10-11)*

Jesus is a greater High Priest in that he is of the order of Melchisedec rather than that of Levi. Mere mention of this fact is made (vv. 6, 10) as the author anticipates it for a later consideration. He must delay that matter, however, seeing that it is a difficult subject to understand, and they "are dull of hearing" (v. 11). In the meantime, he digresses in order to exhort them once again with regard to their arrested development in the Christian calling.

II. THE NEED FOR HIS PRIESTHOOD AFFIRMED (5:12 to 6:20)

1. *The Incompleteness of Their Salvation (5:12 to 6:3)*

This is seen in the fact that the Hebrew Christians possessed incomplete knowledge of the better revelation (v. 12), and they lacked experience in declaring it to others (v. 13f.). How modern is this condition! These two failures combine to result in an incomplete experience of salvation.

The author does not spare his readers in this exhortation. They have been Christians long enough that they should be teaching others; yet they are still in need of teachers themselves. They have not even learned the A B C's, the first principles, of the divine revelation or oracles of God which they are to declare to others. It is of interest to note that Peter (1 Peter 4:11) uses this phrase in reference to God's word to others through Christian people. We see here the stage of their spiritual development.

In the Gospels Jesus invited men to take his yoke

upon them (Matt. 11:29) that they might find *rest* unto their souls. This expression was used to refer to a pupil enrolling in the school of his teacher. As Jesus used it, he referred to their initial experience of faith in becoming Christians or his disciples (students). To be enrolled in his school was to be a redeemed soul; but the idea suggests continued growth in knowledge and its resultant service. The Hebrew Christians had enrolled in the school, but so far they had failed to learn their first lessons. As such they are still babes in Christ, drinking milk when they should be adults masticating strong meat (v. 14). They have not even cut their intellectual teeth in Jesus' school. Because of this they are unskilled in the word of righteousness, the gospel which they should be preaching (v. 13). Our modern churches are full of such infants.

Instead of floundering in infanthood, these Hebrew Christians are urged to go on to adulthood in their Christian venture. The phrase "let us go on" may aptly be rendered "let us be borne on." This is suggestive of the statement in 2:1 *to be flowed by*. Instead of *being flowed by* they are to *be borne on* by the river of God's eternal purpose unto a full or perfect salvation. The word translated "perfection" is derived from a word meaning *mature*. It carries also the teleological idea of going forward to the achievement of a goal. They are not to camp about the "first principles of Christ" (v. 1, Robertson), namely, repentance from dead works, faith toward God, the doctrine of immersions or Jewish ablutions (plural), the laying on of hands, the resurrection, and eternal judgment. These things are mentioned as being the foundation of a building (6:1).

Instead of stopping with the foundation, they are to be busy in constructing the house. It is not clear as to what the author means by these basal elements. Some of

them, such as repentance, faith, the resurrection, and
judgment, appear to be elements in the gospel which
they have believed. The ablutions or immersions do not
refer to Christian baptism. Apparently this is an element
of Judaism which they sought to retain even after their
Christian experience. The laying on of hands could refer
to blessing (Matt. 19:13), healing (Mark 7:32), the be-
stowal of the Holy Spirit (Acts 8:17f.), or their ordina-
tion or separation for a special task (Acts 13:3; 1 Tim.
4:14). Nevertheless, he regards these elements as being
far short of their intended goal, as he urges them to leave
these things to go on to the end for which they are destined. And if God permits or wills it (cf. 1 Cor. 16:7),
as he most certainly does, the writer proposes that they
shall do just that (v. 3).

2. *The Danger of an Incomplete Spiritual Experience* *(vv. 4-8)*

We come now to one of the most difficult passages in
the Bible. For that reason we shall do well to keep before us the entire statement. "For it is impossible for
those who were once enlightened, and have tasted of the
heavenly gift, and were made partakers of the Holy
Ghost, and have tasted the good word of God, and the
powers of the world to come, if they shall fall away, to
renew them again unto repentance; seeing they crucify
to themselves the Son of God afresh, and put him to an
open shame" (vv. 4-6).

Let us be quick to say that this passage presents grave
difficulties. It behooves us to seek its meaning with
reverent humility, to guard against any dogmatic viewpoint that fails to admit the possibility of a contrary
viewpoint being the inspired writer's meaning. Equally
competent scholars disagree. Our conclusions must be
in harmony with the whole teaching of the gospel. My

own view has been arrived at on the basis of the most serious study and thought. It perhaps will not solve for some all the problems involved. But to me it more nearly does so than any other view.

What was the author trying to say to his readers, and through them to us? There is a wide difference of opinion among competent scholars as to this question. Some insist that he is writing to people who have not experienced redemption, warning them that, having come to the knowledge of the truth, if they reject it there is no other means whereby they can be redeemed. Coupling this warning with Paul's statement about falling out of grace into law (Gal. 5:4), they find the author saying that if they reject the grace way of salvation there is no other way to be saved. Frankly, this is the easiest way around the difficulties involved. However, a careful examination of the Scripture passage reveals that the author seems to assume a genuine spiritual experience for his readers. The ones of whom the author writes have been "once for all" (author's translation) enlightened, without reference to further enlightenments. As a result they have tasted of the heavenly gift of redemption and have become *partakers* of the Holy Spirit. He assumes that they had been regenerated.

The problem arises not here, but with the words "shall fall away." Those who admit the fact of a genuine Christian experience are faced with the problem of the possibility that a Christian can be lost again. Those who follow after Armenian theology find here not a problem but support for their position. But the weight of the New Testament teaching is on the side of those who, following Calvinistic theology, insist that one who is genuinely saved can never be lost again. But what are we to do with this particular Scripture passage?

Two general solutions have been offered. On the one

hand it is claimed that the author has in mind a hypothetical case, but one which is in reality impossible.
The Hebrew Christians are in danger, so they say, of
apostatizing from Jesus. To prevent this, the author
poses a situation in which he assumes that a genuine
Christian actually can do this; and says that for such
there is no hope of renewal. But he hastens to remind
them that he is persuaded better things of them (v. 9).
Frankly we do not feel that this satisfies the situation.
If the case be hypothetical, and impossible, why use it
at all? Either you can or you cannot apostatize, that is, be
truly redeemed and later completely lost. Our contention, based upon an abundance of New Testament
teaching, is that a Christian cannot apostatize. The case
of Judas so often referred to is beside the point. One
will strive in vain to show that he was a genuine disciple
of Jesus. The sin against the Holy Spirit, to which some
allude in this connection, is possible only to those who
have never accepted Jesus as Saviour (cf. also 1 John
5:16).

Still others seek a way out of this dilemma by saying
that the thought which the author has in mind is to the
effect that a saving faith will be persevering faith. Only
those who endure to the end shall be saved. In this regard
both Arminians and Calvinists agree. But they part company over the question as to what is meant by persevering
faith. The former contends for a renewing faith in which
a person after being saved may be lost again, only to be
saved once more by an experience of grace. But we would
remind them that that interpretation of this Scripture
passage specifically forbids such. According to it, if persons are lost after being saved, "it is impossible . . . to
renew them again unto repentance" (vv. 4, 6).

On the other hand, the latter group insists upon a
continuing faith which, being genuine, will endure. In

short, if one experiences genuine saving faith, that faith is of such nature that the individual will persevere to the end. With this position we agree, only to ask that if such be the case, then why bother with the question of apostasy at all? This group speaks of the element of struggle in saving faith. But struggle for what? We go back to our original contention that salvation in the sense of redemption is complete and final. The moment a sinner turns in repentance and in genuine faith to the Saviour (John 5:24), that moment he has everlasting life. Everlasting means everlasting without the possibility of it being in any sense temporary—that is, if language means anything.

However, if we agree with the threefold nature of salvation—that it is instantaneous, continuing, and ultimate—the problem would appear to be solved. In that case the author apparently is talking, not of the danger of apostasy in the usual sense of the word, but of the peril of an arrested Christian growth by which these Hebrew Christians are in peril of falling short of their ultimate destiny in Christian behavior and service. We believe that this comes nearer satisfying the situation than any of the other interpretations. With that idea in view let us examine the passage more closely.

Keep in mind the case of the Israelites in the wilderness, a genuinely redeemed people (from bondage) who by *standing off from* God lost the privilege of achieving their destiny. Here, then, we have a parallel in the case of the Hebrew Christians. They, too, have had a genuine spiritual experience (vv. 4-5). But they also are faced with the danger of stopping short of their destiny in Christian growth and service by *standing off from* Jesus (3:12). The word translated "fall away" in verse 6 is *parapesontas* and comes from the Greek verb which carries the root idea of *falling aside* or of deviating from the right path. In the papyri it is used in the sense of breaking the terms of a contract. Dr. James Moffatt tells us that it corresponds to *apostēnai* which we have translated *to stand off from*. He further notes that both these words are used in the Septuagint to translate the Hebrew word which means *deed* with emphasis upon its evil aspect. The idea, then, would seem to be that of *falling aside from* or of *standing off from* Jesus, as the Pioneer of their faith seeks to lead them on in the Christian calling. We cannot repeat too often that this does not have reference to their initial experience in the Christian life but to their part in the greater salvation involving growth in grace, knowledge, and service. Note further that "partakers of the Holy Ghost" may be translated "partners with the Holy Ghost" (cf. 3:1, 14).

Throughout the New Testament the Holy Spirit is pictured as the one who strives through Christians in the work of propagating the gospel. Such an interpretation still leaves us the problem of verse 6. "If they shall fall away [aside] [it is impossible], to renew them again unto repentance; seeing they crucify to themselves the Son of God afresh, and put him to an open shame." But here again we find help in the case of Israel at Kadesh-barnea. When they stood off from God, it was impossible to renew them again unto a change of mind or attitude (real sense of Greek word translated *repentance*) with regard to their destiny, for God decreed that their carcasses should fall in the wilderness. Doubtless they lived to see the day when they wished to repent of their sin of provocation, but God had already said that they should not enter into his *rest*.

The word *crucify afresh* is a mistranslation of the Greek word which, according to Dr. A. T. Robertson, is "the usual verb for crucify in the Old Greek." Thus the Hebrew Christians did not by their sin of *falling aside* crucify Jesus afresh. They simply identified themselves with his crucifiers. Why did the enemies of Jesus crucify him? Was it not in an effort to defeat his eternal purpose? In so doing they actually aided him in achieving it, but that was not their intent. In effect that was the result of the readers of the epistle *falling aside*. In so doing they were being a party to the attitude which would negate the purpose of Jesus' death. The words "open shame" are suggestive both of the fact that Jesus was crucified naked, and of the fact that the multitude in Jerusalem by his crucifixion turned from praising him to cursing him. By their attitude of neglect the Hebrew Christians also were causing the unredeemed multitudes of their day to look with contempt both upon Jesus and upon his redemptive mission for them. Undeveloped Christians in every age carry this same unhappy result from generation to generation.

In concluding his warning, the author cites the example of two pieces of ground, both of which received the same kind of rain (vv. 7-8). The one produced a good harvest and as a result received "blessing from God." The other bore only thorns and briars, and was rejected. It was "nigh unto cursing; whose end is to be burned" (cf. 1 Cor. 3:15). At Kadesh-barnea Israel was "nigh unto cursing." But for the intercession of Moses she would have been destroyed and disinherited. Due to the priestly ministry of Moses, however, that generation escaped such a fate with only the loss of its place in God's redemptive mission. While a disobedient Christian group would be "nigh unto cursing," because of the ministry of their High Priest they would escape that fate to the loss of their fruit in redemptive witnessing. The reference, of course, is to the burning of the product of the land; the land itself was not burned. This is a timeless illustration, applicable to every Christian individual.

3. *The Surety of Full Salvation in Our Great High Priest (vv. 9-20)*

Despite their present attitude of falling short of their world mission, the author hastens to add his word of confidence that his readers will yet go on to the full experience of Christian growth and service for which they are destined (v. 9). Their Christian life thus far has not been entirely devoid of fruit, of which fact God is aware (v. 10). But they should continue in it until they have achieved the desired goal (v. 11). The fact that some, Joshua and Caleb, inherited the promise of God should inspire them to greater effort to that end (v. 12).

The readers of the epistle were not an isolated group whose destiny was bound up within themselves alone. Instead they were but a segment of God's redemptive purpose which began historically with Abraham. To him God had given the promise that in being a blessing he would be the object of God's blessing (Gen. 12:2). Even Abraham was tempted to falter in the course God had given him to travel, but when he found grace to persevere, God reminded him that the promise still stood (vv. 13-15). Because he could swear by no greater God took an oath upon himself, "that in blessing I will bless thee, . . . and in thy seed shall all the nations of the earth be blessed; because thou hast obeyed my voice" (Gen. 22:17-18). Certainly Abraham's trial was equal to theirs. As Abraham's spiritual seed they, too, shall find their place in God's purpose only as they obey him.

The assurance which Abraham received was in God's oath sworn by himself. Among the Israelites a promise was established by two witnesses. In the case of Abraham these two things were God's oath and God's promise, both of which are unchangeable. In the case of Christian people, however, the two *things* which establish the enduring promise are God's oath and God's Son, the fulfilment of his promise. God has verified his oath by the gift of his Son. This oath is further established for God's people by two additional facts—Jesus' death and his continuing priesthood. Therefore they should "lay hold [hold fast] upon the hope set before us" (v. 18) as the goal for their Christian destiny.

The people of God may be tossed about as a ship on a stormy sea, but in their High Priest they have an anchor within the veil to keep them tied to their moorings (vv. 19-20). The figure employed here has reference to a common practice among seafaring people of that day. Whenever a ship came to port and was unable to enter the quiet haven of the harbor because of a sand bar and a low tide, a man in a small boat would take the ship's anchor across the bar and secure it within the safety of the protected harbor. Henceforth, the ship might be called upon to endure the fury of the sea for a period, but after a short time it, too, would, with the rising of the tide, be able to enter the haven of rest, where it completed its assigned task by safely delivering its cargo.

Any given group of Christian people may be called upon for a short while to remain in the world to endure the fury of their present trial. But they have an anchor, *both sure and steadfast,* which has entered the veil of God's presence there to assure their safety until such time that they, too, should receive the full *rest* of God's presence, carrying with them the trophies of their Christian service. In the meantime, secured by their Anchor, they are to continue to bear their cargo, or to render their Christian service, until such time as the Master of the harbor tells them to enter into the haven of rest. This anchor our author identifies as "Jesus, made an high priest for ever after the order of Melchisedec."

III. THE SUPERIORITY OF HIS PRIESTHOOD DEMON-
      STRATED (CHAP. 7)

  1. *The Superior Priesthood Explained (vv. 1-3)*

That Jesus is a priest forever after the order of
Melchisedec is significant, for Melchisedec antedates the
line of Aaron by several hundred years. Thus his line
is God's original priesthood. Aaron's line, therefore, was
a temporary substitute for that which went before and
a type of that which came after it. Melchisedec was a
contemporary of Abraham (v. 2). This strange figure
is mentioned historically only one time (Gen. 14), the
only other reference to him in the Old Testament being
found in the messianic Psalm 110. The occasion of his
first mention is when he received tithes from Abraham
and blessed him. The author of Hebrews identifies him
as King of righteousness and King of peace, the former
being an interpretation of his name, and the latter being
the title ascribed to him in Genesis. Both names are
suggestive of the nature of the kingship of Jesus.

However, the emphasis which figures largely in his
relation to Jesus is seen in the description of him as
being "without father, without mother, without descent
[genealogy], having neither beginning of days, nor end
of life" (v. 3). This reference does not mean that he
actually was not born, nor that he did not die. It simply
means that he appears in the record without mention
of his origin or destiny. He came out of nowhere and he
returned to nowhere. Beyond that the Bible is silent
concerning him.

It is in this light that he is mentioned as being "like
unto the Son of God; . . . a priest continually" (v. 3).
While Jesus is an historical figure with a definite beginning and end of his incarnation, he is but the man-
ifestation in time of the eternal Christ. Unlike the priests

in the line of Levi, he is without beginning of days or end of life. The high priest upon which the Christian relies is eternal; that of Judaism is temporal. Jesus Christ is "the same yesterday, and to day, and for ever" (13:8).

2. *The Superior Priesthood Contrasted with the Lesser One* (*vv. 4-17*)

That the priesthood of Jesus is superior to that of Aaron may be seen in three contrasts between the two lines. In the first place, while the sons of Levi, having been made priests, were instructed to receive tithes from their brethren who were descendants of Abraham, Abraham himself paid tithes to Melchisedec who was a priest *continually*. This fact is further established in the suggestion that Aaron himself paid tithes to Melchisedec in that his father, Levi, was in the loins of Abraham at the time the patriarch paid tithes to the King of Salem. Likewise, Melchisedec blessed Abraham and the line of Aaron, said blessing proving the superiority of the former, since the lesser is always blessed by the greater.

In the second place, the change in the priestly line from that of Levi to Melchisedec indicates the incomplete nature of the former priesthood (vv. 11-12). The Levitical line failed to give man "a perfectly adequate relation to God" (Moffatt). Since this was true, it was necessary that *another kind* (v. 11, the Greek word means not another of the same kind, but of a different kind) of priesthood should be established. The word "change" (v. 12) suggests that in God's choice of another kind of priesthood for his Son, he left the Levitical line off to one side, forever discounted (Robertson). God passed by "the order of Aaron" (v. 11).

In the third place, this truth is supported by the fact that in his choice God even vested his new priesthood in another tribe (vv. 13-15). The old order was out of the tribe of Levi, but the new was out of the tribe of Judah, a tribe which is not mentioned in the law as being a priestly tribe. Jesus, then, is a priest after the order of Melchisedec, not because of a commandment of the law, but by virtue of his endless life (vv. 16-17).

3. *The Need of a Superior Priesthood (vv. 18-20)*

Since the line of Aaron failed to give man "a perfectly adequate relation to God," it was necessary that it should be disannulled or set aside (v. 18). This word is common in the papyri in the legal sense of making void (Robertson). The old line was weak and unprofitable (useless), and therefore it made nothing perfect in that it failed to carry its objects forward to a desired end. Therefore God *brought in* a better hope (6:18-20), or anchor, that through it we might be kept in the line of our destiny until we are brought ultimately into the very presence of God (v. 19). The word for *brought in* is found here only in the New Testament, but it is used by Josephus to express the idea of bringing in a new wife to replace the repudiated one. The meaning is perfectly clear that since the old line failed in its mission, it was necessary to replace it with one that could carry God's people forward in their God-given purpose.

Jesus, therefore, is the guarantee (v. 22) that God's promise sworn to by himself (6:13) is to be carried out. The redemptive purpose of God did not find fruition in the succession of priests (v. 23) under the old dispensation, whether we think of it in terms of redemption or ultimate destiny. But in the intercession of the unchanging priesthood of Jesus, his people may be saved "to the uttermost" (v. 25). It is not clear whether the author has in mind the idea of degree or that of time. Probably both are included. He saves or redeems eternally from any depth of sin, but he also enables the redeemed to realize the full degree of salvation in its threefold sense—instantaneous, continual, and ultimate. This he does through his continuous intercession before the throne of grace. Because he has become "consecrated for evermore" (v. 28), the idea being that of fulfilment of a predestined purpose, he is able to carry the Christian forward to the redemptive work for which he is called.

FOR REVIEW AND FURTHER STUDY

1. Who is the High Priest of the new covenant? Were the temptations of Jesus real? What specific temptation of Jesus is mentioned in the Gospels? What is meant by Jesus being made *perfect*? What was the immediate temptation facing the Hebrew Christians?

2. What was the spiritual condition of the Hebrew Christians? Is it possible for a genuine Christian to apostatize? What was the danger facing the Hebrew Christians?

3. Who was Melchisedec? In what way does Jesus correspond to him in his priesthood? Out of what tribe does Jesus' high priesthood spring?

4. What is the meaning of Jesus' high priesthood to us?

5

THE COVENANT
WITH GOD

[Chap. 8]

In the opening verses of chapter 8 our author passes to the next phase of his argument by summarizing the entire comparison of the high priesthood of Jesus as over against that of Aaron (vv. 1-6). The climax of this comparison is in reality the base upon which the entire relationship rests—that of a covenant between God and his people (v. 6) whereby the redemptive purpose of God was to be set into operation. From before the foundation of the world that purpose had been an ideal in the heart of God. In his covenant with Abraham it was set forth as the mission of the seed of the patriarch. Through the witness of that seed in all ages to come, the ideal was to become a reality. For such to be true there must be a method or means by which it could be accomplished. God has ordained that his work shall be done through human instruments which are dedicated to his purpose and empowered by his presence. To that end the author of Hebrews invites his readers to consider their place in the eternal purpose of God's redemptive mission, said place being set forth in their covenant.

I. The Significance of the Old Covenant (v. 9)

1. The Fact of the Covenant (Ex. 6:7)

The covenant idea looms large in the life of all ancient

peoples. The Hebrew word for covenant is *berith* (Greek, *diathēkē*) which comes from a verb that is akin to the Assyrian word *barû* meaning to bind. A covenant therefore was binding. But the Hebrew word itself comes from the root idea "to cut," and is expressive of the custom of cutting an agreement in stone. Involved also may be the practice of cutting the body to obtain blood in order to seal the pact agreed upon by the covenanting parties. Covenants were in fact legal agreements (Heb. 9:16f.) which when sealed were considered as binding upon both parties involved, and could not be broken without penalty.

In the history of God's dealings with his people the covenant idea has a prominent place. Examination of the Scriptures reveals that God made covenants with Adam (Gen. 3:15), Noah (Gen. 9:8ff.), and Abraham (Gen. 12:1-3), the last of which he renewed with Isaac (Gen. 26:2ff.) and Jacob (Gen. 28:13ff.). Indeed, throughout the Old Testament we find God making covenants with various individuals and groups. We have seen that God's covenant with Abraham was basic in his redemptive purpose for all men (Gen. 6:13ff.).

It is clear, however, that in our present passage the author has in mind the covenant which God made through Moses with Israel (Ex. 6:7f.). When Moses was in the midst of his contest with Pharaoh, God instructed him to say unto the children of Israel, "I am the Lord, and I will bring you out from under the burdens of the Egyptians, and I will rid you out of their bondage, and *I will redeem you* [author's italics] with a stretched out arm, and with great judgments: and I will take you to me for a people, and I will be to you a God: . . . And I will bring you in unto the land, concerning the which I did swear to give it to Abraham, to Isaac, and to Jacob; and I will give it you for an heritage: I am the Lord."

Herein we find the basic elements of God's covenant which he made with Abraham, and which becomes clearer in his pronouncement to Moses. It is a covenant of redemption and fellowship. The redemption God is about to achieve; the fellowship will be established and explained following their redemption from the bondage of Egypt.

2. *The Founding of the Old Covenant (Ex. 19:4-7)*

Three months after God's redemption of his people, Moses led them (cf. Heb. 8:9) to the region of Mount Sinai. There God actually founded the covenant which he had promised in Egypt, a covenant which involved their redemption which he has already accomplished (v. 4). Upon that basis ("therefore," v. 5) he proceeded to enter into a covenant relation with them. It is significant for our understanding of Hebrews to remember that God covenants only with a redeemed people.

"Now therefore, if ye will obey my voice indeed, and keep my covenant, then ye shall be a peculiar treasure unto me above all people: for all the earth is mine: and ye shall be unto me a kingdom of priests, and an holy nation" (vv. 5-6). It is evident that this is a covenant of fellowship. Although God owns all peoples of the earth, he purposes to enter into a special relationship with Israel. In an especial manner he has redeemed them from bondage. But beyond that God engages himself for the purpose of making of them a people different (peculiar) from all other peoples. This decision on the part of God is not one of idle caprice. It does not grow out of love for Israel to the exclusion of all other nations. Rather it is because God loves all nations that he chooses one particular nation to be a *peculiar treasure* unto him.

That this choice is not without purpose is seen in the fact that in return for Israel's privilege she is to bear a responsibility. She is to be a "kingdom of priests, and an holy nation." A priest was one who stood between God and man to bring them together in redemptive fellowship. Israel, therefore, was to be a priest-nation whose function was to make God known to the other nations of the earth, and to bring them together for a fellowship of redemption and service. As such she was to be a *holy nation*. The basic meaning of the word "holy" is that of being set apart in dedication to the service of God. While the sense of sinlessness came to be attached to it, it did so only as a reflection of the character of God. Even sinful people were sometimes regarded among pagan peoples as being holy in that they were dedicated to the service of their god. Thus Israel is to be a nation dedicated to God for a priestly ministry to all other nations.

It is well to remember that every covenant was conditioned upon the faithfulness of the two parties involved. The one who originated the pact usually was the superior of the two, and, therefore, was bound only by the good faith of the one who received it. This is the significance of the words "if" and "then" in Exodus 19:5. *If* Israel will become a priest-nation dedicated to God's redemptive purpose, *then* they shall be a peculiar treasure unto God above all other people. Only as Israel shouldered the responsibility could she share the privilege. It is well to remember this as we think not only of Israel but of ourselves in the economy of God. As to Abraham so God said to Israel, and to us, that he will bless only as his people are a blessing. Beyond that God is under no obligation.

3. *The Ministry Under the Old Covenant (Ex. 19:8; 24:1-8)*

This covenant relation was accepted by Israel (19:8), and was later sealed in the blood of sacrifice (Ex. 24: 1-8).

In so doing the agreement became binding upon both parties. Under this covenant God agreed to provide Israel with a home (Ex. 6:8) which was to serve as a base of operation in God's redemptive purpose. The strategic location of Canaan may be seen by referring to any map of the ancient world. It was literally a bridge between the desert and the sea over which the traffic of the ancient world moved. From this central location Israel was to move out into all the inhabited earth as she carried the redemptive message of God to all peoples.

II. THE FAILURE OF THE OLD COVENANT (vv. 7-8, 13)

1. *The Cause of Failure (vv. 7-8)*

Returning to the Epistle to the Hebrews, we find that the old covenant failed to achieve the purpose for which God made it. "For if that first covenant had been fault-less" (v. 7)—here the author uses a Greek condition of the second class which implies that the old covenant was not without fault. But he hastens to add that the fault lay not with God but with Israel: "For finding fault with *them*" [author's italics] (v. 8). God was ever ready, even anxious, to keep his part of the bargain in regarding Israel as a peculiar treasure, but Israel failed to keep her side of the agreement to be a dedicated priest-nation.

The Old Testament ever echoes this tragic truth. First, Israel refused to enter her land of destiny. When the second generation did go in, they disregarded God's admonition to rid the land of paganism. Instead of the priest-nation evangelizing Canaan, she was paganized by the Canaanites. The book of Judges may well be sum-marized in these words: Israel sinned; God punished; Israel repented; God delivered; Israel sinned. Generation after generation God sent his prophets to call Israel back to her mission, only to have them mistreated or slain by an obstinate people. Israel was ever ready to claim her privilege, but never ready to assume her responsibility. Instead she became proud, arrogant, and exclusive. In return, the peoples to whom she was to minister echoed their own pride and arrogance—and regarded Israel as repulsive.

It is well at this point to notice the basic cause of Israel's failure. Recall that the twofold dignity of man was his mastery in material things and his mission in spiritual matters. Likewise, note that to Abraham God promised material blessings only as a means by which he should carry out his spiritual mission. But Israel made the mistake that has been repeated by God's people through the ages—she forgot her spiritual mission in her mad pursuit toward material and political power. A clear example of this is seen in 1 Samuel 8. Since her constitution as a people, Israel had lived under a theocracy, wherein she was ruled by those directly appointed of God. Even after her settlement in Canaan, she ever looked with envy upon the pagan people about her, forgetting the true nature of her relation to God. Finally, this envy came to the surface when the elders of Israel came to the aging Samuel with a request. "Behold, thou art old, and thy sons walk not in thy ways: now make us a king to judge us like all the nations" (v. 5). Despite the warning of God through Samuel they persisted, "Nay; but we will have a king over us; *that we also may be like all the nations;* and that our king may judge us, and go out before us, and *fight our battles*" [author's italics] (vv. 19f.).

Two things stand out in this request. First, they wanted to be like their pagan neighbors instead of being a *peculiar* treasure unto God. Unlike Moses they valued the glamor of the world more than their invisible mission for God. Like the disciples of Jesus they reckoned greatness by the pagan standard of the number of those who served them rather than by the divine standard of the number whom they could serve (Matt. 20:25-28). Second, they thought in terms of military conquest rather than in terms of a spiritual crusade. They stood off from God while they sought a king to go before them to fight their battles. Although God knew the tragic consequence of their request yet he granted it. The dignity of man is such that he is permitted to make his choices, even though they may run contrary to the will of God.

These two attitudes continued to characterize Israel throughout her history. The period of the kings of Israel tells the sad story of material and political conquest to the neglect of her true mission. Instead of becoming a priest-nation for spiritual endeavor, she enlarged her boundaries and enriched her coffers at the terrible price of mingled hatred and fear on the part of her neighbors. The zenith of her worldly glory came in the reign of Solomon who, through military conquest, economic prowess, and political marriage, extended her borders and deepened her sin. The bitter fruit of his reign was a divided kingdom which became the unhappy victim of those toward whom her spiritual mission was directed. In pursuit of her false destiny in political and material spheres, Israel failed to achieve her true destiny of spiritual greatness.

2. The Climax of Their Failure (v. 13; cf. Matt. 21:28-46)

This attitude deepened to such an extent that when Jesus appeared on the scene, there was no one in Israel, not even John the Baptist, who regarded the kingdom of God in its true light. So deep-seated was their vision of worldly grandeur and power that even their conception of the Messiah was devoid of spiritual significance. For this reason the nation which was to have been the peculiar treasure of God rejected the Messiah in whom God's redemptive purpose was to have been achieved, said rejection heralding the end of the covenant which God had made with his people (Heb. 8:13).

The climax of Israel's rejection and God's disavowal of the old covenant is recorded in Matthew 21:28-46. When it became evident that the Jews would not honor their covenant relation, Jesus taught in two parables the terrible and final result of their rebellion. The first of these parables is that of the two sons (vv. 28-32). A certain man (God) had two sons, one of which (Israel) agreed to work in his vineyard, but failed to do so. The other son (Gentiles) at first refused to do so, but belatedly *changed his mind* and went to work in the vineyard. (The word is the same Greek word usually translated *repent*. Here we have the true rendering of its root meaning.)

Having given a foregleam of the final issue of the matter, Jesus proceeded to give at length the parable of the wicked husbandmen (vv. 33-39). In this illustration Jesus pictures a householder (God) who owned a vineyard (God's redemptive purpose) which he had rented out to husbandmen (Israel). Repeatedly he sent his servants (prophets, etc.) to collect his rent (the fruit of their redemptive endeavor). In every instance, the husbandmen refused to respond to the appeal of the servants, beating one, stoning others, and, in one instance, killing another. Finally the owner sent his son (Jesus), thinking that they would surely respond to him. Instead, they plotted and killed him that they might receive for themselves his inheritance, which they regarded only in a material sense.

Having completed his parables, Jesus proceeded to apply them. "When the lord therefore of the vineyard cometh, what will he do unto those husbandmen?" (v.

40). The Jewish leaders to whom Jesus' words were directed as the spiritual heads of the nation replied, "He will miserably destroy those wicked men, and will let out his vineyard unto other husbandmen, which shall render him the fruits in their seasons" (v. 41). To this Jesus replied in ominous words, "Did ye never read in the scriptures, The stone which the builders rejected, the same is become the head of the corner: ... Therefore say I unto you, *The kingdom of God shall be taken from you, and given to a nation bringing forth the fruits thereof* [author's italics]. And whosoever shall fall on this stone shall be broken: but on whomsoever it shall fall, it will grind him to powder" (vv. 42ff.). That this truth found its mark is seen in the final word, "And when the chief priests and Pharisees had heard his parables, they perceived that he spake of them" (v. 45). Even then their rebellion would have evolved in murder had they not feared the people (v. 46). Let God's people in every age read these words—and tremble!

3. *The Consequence of Their Failure (1 Peter 2:4-10)*

The significance of Jesus' words may be seen as we turn to this remarkable statement of the apostle Peter. We may be certain that he had in mind both the passage in Exodus 19 and Matthew 21 (cf. also Jer. 31:31-34). After referring to Jesus as the cornerstone who is precious to those who believe, and is a stone of stumbling to those who are disobedient to God's will, he says of his readers who are Christian people, "But ye are a chosen generation; a royal priesthood, an holy nation, a peculiar people; that ye should shew forth the praises of him who hath called you out of darkness into his marvellous light: which in time past were not a people, but are now the people of God: which had not obtained mercy, but now have obtained mercy." The similarity of language here and in the aforementioned passages cannot be regarded as accidental. The definite implication is to the effect that the Christian people stand in the same relation to God as that promised to Israel. When the latter failed, God turned to the former.

Many conscientious interpreters have erred in supposing God's covenant with Israel to be a permanent one. However, we must recall that the covenant relation was posited on Israel's obedience in assuming the responsibility to be used of God in world redemption. Failing in this, she lost the covenant which God, in turn, gave to a people who in time past did not even exist, but who came into being through the redemptive ministry of Christ. If the permanency of Israel's relationship be insisted upon, let it be remembered that John the Baptist reminded the Pharisees that they were not to regard their relation to Abraham's seed as a racial but as a spiritual one (Matt. 3:9). Furthermore, Paul's reference to Israel in Romans 9-11 involves the same thought. "For they are not all Israel, which are of Israel" (9:6). The seed of Abraham are a spiritual seed apart from the flesh (9:7ff.). In short, we as Christians are the true seed of Abraham to whom the covenant pertains. When national Israel failed, she lost her covenant relation to a spiritual Israel which should bring forth the fruits thereof.

III. THE GIVING OF THE NEW COVENANT (vv. 6, 8-12)

1. *The Promise of the New Covenant (vv. 8, 10; cf. Jer. 31:31-34)*

More than six hundred years before Jesus was born, God promised a new covenant for his people. Looking back, we recall that Israel throughout her history had wasted her energy in an effort to achieve her destiny in the material and political realm. This effort reached its zenith under Solomon. Following his death the kingdom was divided. Because of the Northern Kingdom's (Israel) continued rebellion against God's will, even to the point of idolatry, that kingdom fell to the Assyrians in 722 B.C. For more than one hundred years afterward, the Southern Kingdom (Judah) followed largely the same path until in 605 B.C. she fell before the Babylonians, her utter destruction coming in 587 B.C.

Late in Judah's history Jeremiah sought to call her back to her destiny. Finally, when it became clear that she would not heed, God spoke to Jeremiah of a new covenant which he would make with his people. "Behold, the days come, saith the Lord, that I will make a new covenant with the house of Israel, and with the house of Judah: not according to the covenant that I made with their fathers in the day that I took them by the hand to bring them out of the land of Egypt; which my covenant they brake, although I was an husband unto them, saith the Lord: but this shall be the covenant that I will make with the house of Israel; After those days, saith the Lord, I will put my law in their inward parts, and write it in their hearts; and will be their God, and they shall be my people. And they shall teach no more every man his neighbour, and every man his brother, saying, Know the Lord; for they shall all know me, from the least of them unto the greatest of them, saith the Lord: for I will forgive their iniquity, and I will remember their sin no more" (31:31-34).

It is to this event that our author refers when he says, "For finding fault [present middle participle, indicating a repeated action] with them, he saith, Behold, the days come, saith the Lord, when I will make a new covenant with the house of Israel and with the house of Judah" (Heb. 8:8). Note that God regards Israel as a unit, although the Northern Kingdom had long since ceased to exist as a people.

This new covenant will not be written upon tables of stone, but will be "into their mind" and "in their hearts" (v. 10). It will be spiritual and inward, not fleshly and outward. It will be a covenant of grace and not of law. This new covenant will be written in their intellect or moral understanding. Aristotle uses this phrase to refer to all of one's intellect. Furthermore, it will be engraved upon their hearts, the seat of man's personal life. These two terms, mind and heart, cover the whole of man's inward nature, implying a closer relationship and a greater responsibility.

2. *The Sealing of the New Covenant (v. 6)*

Although this new covenant was promised through Jeremiah, it did not become operative until Jesus came. Recall that God covenants only with a redeemed people. As Israel had to be redeemed out of Egypt in order to be eligible to enter into her covenant, so did his people who in former times were not a people have to be redeemed by the death of Jesus before they could be able to enter into a covenant with God. This new people was not confined to any one nation, but was to come out of every kindred, tongue, and nation (Rev. 5:9; 7:9).

As the covenant with Israel was sealed in blood, so was the new covenant sealed in the blood of Jesus (Heb. 9:18ff.; cf. Matt. 26:28). Thus he became the Mediator of this new covenant. The word "mediator" is from a Greek word *(mesitēs)* meaning middle man or arbitrator. It was commonly used for an intermediary in civil transactions. Thus Jesus was the Intermediary between God and man as they entered into an agreement to become partners in world redemption. In essence, then, when an individual accepts Christ's atoning sacrifice for his redemption, at the same time he accepts the conditions of this covenant relation. More is involved in it than

merely the initial act of salvation. It also entails the
further responsibility of going on to a full salvation
which involves Christian service. Still the promise to
the Christian, as to Abraham and to Israel, involves both
privilege and responsibility.

3. *The Ministry Under the New Covenant (vv. 11f.)*

The deeper sense of this new covenant may be seen in
the nature of its ministry. Under the new covenant every
believer is a priest. Under the old covenant only the
scribe could understand the minutiae of the law, which
he was charged to teach to the people. But under the new
covenant "they shall not teach every man his neighbour
[fellow-citizen], and every man his brother, saying, Know
the Lord: for all shall know me, from the least to the
greatest" (v. 11). We have here a play on two Greek
words regarding knowledge. The first is a knowledge
received from experience or teaching, as that which
comes from outside one. The second is an intuitive
knowledge which comes from within. In short, under the
new covenant the Christian shall possess a knowledge of
God which comes from his heart.

However, this play upon words further suggests the
ministry of the Christian to those who are without that
intuitive knowledge. While every man has the witness of
God in his heart (Rom. 1:19), he can come to have that
intuitive knowledge of God as Redeemer only as saved
men bring to bear upon him the experiential knowledge
of God in salvation. Here, then, is the mission of every
Christian. Whether it be to his neighbor or to those in
lands afar, he is to share his knowledge of God until it
shall cover the earth as the waters cover the sea (Hab.
2:14). Under the old covenant which was ready to vanish
away (v. 13), this ideal was not realized. Under the new
covenant we must not fail.

For Review and Further Study

1. What is a covenant? Read Exodus 19:1-7. What was involved in the Mosaic covenant?

2. Why did the old covenant fail? What was Israel's destiny? What false destiny did she pursue? Compare Exodus 19:4-7; Matthew 21:28-46; 1 Peter 2:4-10.

3. Read Jeremiah 31:31-34. What was the difference between the old covenant and the new covenant? How was the new covenant sealed? What is the Christian's ministry under the new covenant?

4. Do we face the same fate which befell Israel if we refuse to live up to the new covenant?

6

REDEEMED FOR SERVICE

[9:1-12]

THE SANCTUARY of God has ever been central in the
development and service of his people. The Temple in
Jerusalem which was about to pass away was in reality an
intermediate institution between the temporal tabernacle and the heavenly temple which were identified with
the ministry of Aaron and Jesus. Therefore the author
of Hebrews spends no time with it beyond the veiled
reference in 8:13. His interest is centered in the tabernacle which was the type and in the heavenly sanctuary
which was the fulfilment of the type. With these figures
he continues his comparison between the temporary
high priesthood of Aaron and the eternal high priesthood of Jesus. Implied but not stated is the theme which
permeates the epistle, that as the latter is greater than
the former, so should the children under the new covenant exceed those under the old in fulfilling the destiny
which has been given to them.

I. THE WORLDLY SANCTUARY (vv. 1-5; cf. Ex. 25ff.)

1. *The Meaning of the Tabernacle (vv. 1-2a)*

The symbol of the old covenant was the tabernacle
and its divine services. In reference to it the author has
in mind particularly its ministry in the wilderness before
Israel's entrance into Canaan, that reference implying
that its services failed to bring its people into the full
experience of their divine mission.

The tabernacle (Ex. 25ff.) was little more than a large ornate tent oblong in shape. It was made by Moses with gifts from the people (25:2-7), and according to definite instructions which he received from Jehovah (25:9). The tabernacle itself was located within the outer court, a covered area in which was located the altar of sacrifice and the laver, used by the priests for ablutions before entering the holy place. We shall not labor the text by describing the tabernacle itself. The point of the author is related more to the meaning of the tabernacle, its contents, and its services. Suffice it to repeat at this time that the tabernacle was a symbol of the presence of God in the midst of his people (25:8). This is the significance of the tent which could be dismantled and moved about by the people in their wilderness wanderings. Thus they were constantly reminded that they were not alone, for their God was with them whithersoever they went.

2. *The Holy Place (v. 2b)*

The actual tabernacle was divided into two sections known as the *holy place* and the *holy of holies,* or the most holy place. Into the first, called sometimes the tabernacle of the congregation, the priests went daily for their service to God. Into the second went only the high priest to meet with God, and that once each year on the Day of Atonement.

As the tabernacle itself symbolized the presence of God among his people, so did the various articles of furniture carry particular meanings which were suggestive of God's relation to them. As the priest passed through the outer veil on the east into the holy place, he saw the table of shewbread on the north, made of acacia wood overlaid with gold. On it were twelve cakes of shewbread, one for each of the twelve tribes; these were renewed by the priests once each week. By this bread the Israelites were reminded that it was God who sustained life, and that they were to dedicate to him the life thus sustained. On the priest's left, or to the south, stood the candlestick made of pure gold. It was placed there for the practical purpose of giving light; but it further symbolized the fact that God was their light, and that they, in turn, were to be a light to the whole world (cf. Matt. 5: 14-16). Before the inner veil to the west stood the altar of incense overlaid with gold from which rose the continuously burning incense as a symbol of the prayers of the people which went up to God.

3. *The Holy of Holies (vv. 3-5)*

This section of the tabernacle which our author calls the "Holiest of all" stood within the veil, suggesting the inapproachable nature of God. Through this veil only the high priest might enter, and that once each year. Within the veil was seen the ark of the covenant, a small container overlaid within and without with pure gold.

Within the ark had been placed three objects which were a testimony concerning God's relation to his people. There was the pot of manna (Ex. 16) which constantly reminded the people of God's sustaining care during their trials in the wilderness. Also, the ark contained Aaron's rod which budded (Num. 17:10), as an abiding testimony to his divine appointment as the high priest of Israel whose ministry preserved and presented them as acceptable before God for his service. The third object was the two tables of stone on which were written the covenant of Jehovah with his people (Ex. 24:12; 25:16). This was a perpetual memorial of the covenant relation which God made with his people and of the redemption which they had accepted (Ex. 19:5-9; 24:1-8). Over this ark was laid the mercy seat, a slab of pure gold, which was to be the meeting place between God and Moses (Ex.

25:22). Hovering above the mercy seat were the cherubim whose wings covered the mercy seat and whose eyes were focused upon it. These suggested the presence of God as accessible in mercy.

It is of interest to note that our author places the altar of incense within the veil, while the Old Testament apparently places it outside (Ex. 30). Many theories have been advanced in an effort to explain this. Dr. A. T. Robertson leaves it unsettled, suggesting that it may have been located within the veil. The account in Exodus 30 is vague on the matter. Dr. Moffatt observes that the Septuagint is not clear as to the location of the altar of incense. However, the record does say that Aaron was to light the altar of incense daily (Ex. 30:7), which he could not have done were it within the veil. Dr. Robertson further points out that it is uncertain whether the word used by our author should be translated *censer* or *altar of incense*. However, in the Septuagint, which was used by our author, it means censer. It may, therefore, refer to the censer which Aaron took with him annually when he went into the holy of holies. At any rate the altar of incense was used for the ritual within the veil. It was this thought apparently which was uppermost in the author's mind.

II. The Ministry in the Sanctuary (vv. 6-10)

1. *The Daily Ministry (v. 6)*

According to the law of God the priests were to minister daily in the "first tabernacle." Whenever the people brought their individual sacrifices for individual sins or uncleanness, the priests were to minister before the Lord for them. In addition there were those set occasions throughout the year when they were to offer sacrifices unto Jehovah (Num. 28-29). "Day by day" they were to offer a continual burnt offering (28:3). On each sabbath day (28:9), the new year (28:11), the Passover (28:16), the day of first fruits (28:26), the feast of trumpets (29:1), and at various other stated occasions throughout the year, the priests offered sacrifices prescribed for the occasion.

The emphasis, of course, is upon the succession of sacrifices offered by a succession of priests generation after generation. One can sense the endless repetition which seemed to lead nowhere, as "the priests went always into the first tabernacle, accomplishing the service of God" (Heb. 9:6). Furthermore we are reminded of the inefficacy of animal sacrifice as a means of purifying the people for their service to God.

2. *The Annual Ministry (v. 7)*

In addition to all this, there was the annual ministry rendered by the high priest on the Day of Atonement, "throughout your generations" (v. 7; cf. Ex. 30:10). This day was the tenth day of the seventh month of their year (Lev. 16:29). On this day the high priest, after washing himself, put on his linen garments called "holy garments." He then brought two kids of the goats of the congregation and presented them before the Lord at the door of the tabernacle of the congregation. On these goats were cast lots, one to indicate which was to be sacrificed unto the Lord, and the other to choose which was to be the scapegoat for the people. Having done this, he took a bullock and sacrificed it for his own sins and those of his house. Then, taking a censer of burning coals from off the altar, together with sweet incense and the blood of the bullock, he entered through the veil into the holy of holies. There he put the incense in the fire that the cloud of the incense might cover the mercy seat so that he might not die. Thus he could enter the presence of God only in prayer. Then, taking the blood of the bullock, with his finger he sprinkled it once upon the mercy seat, and before the mercy seat seven times.

Having made atonement for his own sins, he proceeded to make atonement for the sins of the people. Slaying the goat on which the lot of the Lord fell, he sprinkled the mercy seat with its blood as he did with the bullock's blood. Then he took the blood of both out into the holy place and put it upon the horns of the altar. Thus he cleansed the holy place and the tabernacle of the congregation. Having done this, he took the scapegoat and symbolically placed upon its head the sins of the people. This goat was led away into the wilderness to die. Then the high priest entered again into the tabernacle of the congregation where he put off his garments and washed his body. Leaving the garments there and putting on his other clothes, he went out and offered burnt offerings for himself and the people. The remains of the sacrifices were carried outside the camp and burned (cf. Heb. 13: 11). The man who led the scapegoat away, together with the one who burned the residue of the sacrifices, washed their clothes and bathed their bodies, after which they were allowed to re-enter the camp.

All this was highly symbolic, the meaning of which is quite evident. While not stated in the Scripture passage, it was customary for the high priest to announce to the people that atonement for their sins had been made for that year. They, in turn, went everywhere carrying the glad news.

3. *The Parable in the Ministry (vv. 8-10)*

Having referred to the above ministries, the author of Hebrews hastens to remind his readers that the tabernacle and its services were but a parable ("figure," v. 9) of the heavenly sanctuary and the ministry of their High Priest. The necessary endless repetition of the sacrifices denoted their inability to reach down into the conscience of the people to effect a permanent change in them. They were temporary ordinances which must give way to a new order or reformation (v. 10). The endless rites and ceremonies of Judaism called for something more.

Several years ago I was invited to preach to a Jewish congregation. Before the sermon they went through their prescribed ritual. As I listened I felt the utter emptiness of it all. Somehow I wanted to cry out to them, "There is something more!" That was the sensation of our author as he pondered the emptiness of the old and the fulness of the new.

III. THE HEAVENLY SANCTUARY (vv. 11-12)

1. *The Fulfilment of the Worldly Sanctuary* (v. 11b)

The significance of the earthly tabernacle is seen in the fact that it is an antitype of the heavenly sanctuary (9:24). God showed Moses the type or model of heavenly realities, and he, in turn, made an antitype of that model.

As the worldly tabernacle was a constant reminder of God's presence among them for their personal redemption and service, so is the heavenly sanctuary our assurance that God in Christ is among us as our Redeemer and Leader in our Christian growth and ministry.

While our author's chief interest lies within the veil, the typology includes more. Every piece of furniture in the Mosaic tabernacle corresponds to an element in Christ's ministry for us. The shewbread is suggestive of Jesus as our constant source of strength (John 6:35). As he sustains our lives, we, in turn, are to dedicate them to his service. The light of the candlestick reminds us that Jesus is the Light of the world (John 8:12), and that from his light we are to receive enlightenment that we in turn might become the light of the world (Matt. 5:14). The altar of incense is symbolic of prayer, and the incense above the mercy seat reminds us of the intercessory prayers of Jesus by which we have an approach to God (7:25). The contents of the ark of the covenant are no less suggestive. The holy manna reminds us that Christ is God's provision for us to sustain us in our trials. Aaron's rod is but a model of our inner witness that Jesus is our eternal High Priest appointed of God. The tables of stone point forward to him who is the fufilment of God's law (Matt. 5:17). The mercy seat with the over-shadowing cherubim testifies that God in Christ has met with us for our redemption (2 Cor. 5:19).

As Aaron ministered temporarily outside the veil only to enter within the veil to effect his ministry in God's atoning work, so the Word became flesh and dwelt (tabernacled) among us (John 1:14) for a little while, that he might enter through the veil into the heavenly holy of holies, where his presence at the right hand of God assures us of our redemption in him.

2. *The High Priest of the Heavenly Sanctuary (v. 11a)*

However, the text is quite clear to the effect that the author's primary interest lies in the fact that Christ is the fulfilment of the ministry of the high priest on the Day of Atonement. As such he is identified with man (4:15) yet has his priesthood from God (5:5). He has an unchangeable high priesthood in contrast to the temporal office of Aaron (7:23f.). Over against the sinful nature of the old order, he is "holy, harmless, undefiled, separate from sinners, and made higher than the heavens" (7:26). For Christ is "an high priest of good things to come" (v. 11), who ministers in a tabernacle not made with hands (cf. Acts 17:24). "Neither by the blood of goats and calves, but by his own blood he entered in once [once for all] into the holy place, having obtained eternal redemption for us" (v. 12). The author proceeds to enlarge upon this summary, a matter to which we shall return in the next chapter.

3. The Ministry in the Heavenly Sanctuary (v. 12)

For the present let us focus our attention upon the phrase "eternal redemption." Note first of all that the redemption which Christ provides is eternal in contrast to the temporal nature of the former as is seen in the annual repetition of the sacrifice. This refers not so much to the result as to the means. Being imperfect, the sacrifice under the old covenant must be repeated, while that of Jesus is effective without repetition.

What does the author mean by *redemption?* This question has contained the minds of theologians through the ages. We cannot accept the medieval concept of God paying a ransom to Satan for the souls of men. But the language here and in Matthew 20:28, where a stronger form of the same word is used, definitely infers that a ransom was paid for man's redemption. We can better understand this truth when we remember that God made man for his fellowship of love and service. It is not an anthropomorphism to say that following the creation of his material universe and the animals therein, God was lonely. Being a Person, he found no fellowship with material things or with brutish creatures. As man was lonely without woman, so was God lonesome without man. Being a God of love, he needed someone upon whom he could bestow his love, and who in turn could respond to it. Thus "God created man in his own image" (Gen. 1:27). It was not an image of physical likeness but of spiritual kinship. As such, God could enter into fellowship with man.

In order to be capable of responding to this relationship, man was made free—free to love, free to serve, free to choose. For this threefold fellowship to be real there had to be an opposite from God to which man might choose to give his love and loyalty. It was in this regard that Satan entered the picture. In the garden of Eden Satan literally stole man from God. He stole his love and his loyalty. In making his choice between God's word and Satan's word, man violated the fellowship which he had with God. Being a God of love and mercy, Jehovah could not let the matter go at that. Being a God of holiness, he could not ignore man's sin. Somehow the fellowship must be restored (Heb. 2:10). God must redeem man back into the mutual relationship with himself. And since God was the injured party, he must make the approach to man (cf. Matt. 18:15).

In this approach God might have chosen any one of several routes. He might have redeemed man by power, but it would have been an incomplete redemption. You can coerce man's body but not his heart or his will. You can force a man to obey you or else take the consequences. But you cannot force him to love you. That must be achieved in another way. Man's fellowship of love and service must be a matter of man's will and not that of God alone. Furthermore, God might have employed animal sacrifice, as he did. But this method was incomplete in that it involved only the sacrifice of dumb brutes which, in itself, was powerless to elicit a proper response from the soul of man. Again, he might have used human sacrifice. This might have produced a limited response in the heart of man. But other men, being sinful, could not serve for the atonement of still other men of like nature.

Therefore, to achieve his proposed purpose, God was faced with a dilemma. His holiness must be satisfied. Since the wages of sin is death, someone must die to bridge the chasm between God and man. But such a victim must within himself be not only soulful but sinless. Finding none among men who was worthy, there remained only for God himself to be both "just, and the justifier" (Rom. 3:26). *God must pay the ransom, and it must be paid to himself!*

As someone has fittingly said, animal blood is impotent to cleanse man from sin in that it is nonmoral. Human blood cannot do so because it is immoral. Only the blood of Christ could suffice because it is moral. In the person of his Son, therefore, who became both the sacrifice and the sacrificer, or high priest, "He entered in once into the holy place, having obtained eternal redemption for us" (v. 12).

But divine redemption is not from something to nothing. While God made man for himself, it was not simply for the purpose of idle adoration. Beyond the redemption of an individual is the larger redemption of a race. When God chose Israel, it was not a mere matter of choosing one people to the neglect of all others. In every instance of choice on the part of God, there is seen the element of purposeful selection.

Take the example of Israel to which reference has already been made. In Romans 9 Paul expresses his desire that all Israel shall be saved. We have already seen that Paul is careful to distinguish between a racial Israel and a spiritual Israel. "For they are not all Israel, which are of Israel" (v. 6). Simply because one is of the seed of Abraham does not imply that he is a part of the Israel of the covenant. Abraham had two sons, Isaac and Ishmael, but in the line of Isaac, the younger, ran the redemptive purpose of God. Isaac had two sons, Jacob (Israel) and Esau. Again, although Israel was the younger, the promise was through him. Here Paul quotes from Malachi, "Jacob have I loved, but Esau have I hated" (v. 13). This was not an arbitrary decision on God's part. The words *love* and *hate* refer not to an emotion, but contain the element of a measured choice. Because of Esau's nature he was unfit for the redemptive purpose of God. Because Jacob, an unlikely candidate at the time, possessed within his nature the elements which fitted him for God's purpose, he was chosen over against his elder brother. In turn, the descendants of Jacob (Israel) were chosen to be a priest-nation in the cause of world redemption.

IV. THE EARTHLY MISSION OF THE HEAVENLY SANCTUARY (vv. 10, 12)

1. *The Time of Reformation (v. 10)*

We have seen in chapter 5 that this element of purposeful choice led God to reject Israel in favor of the people of Christ. When it became evident to him that Israel, the elder, was not willing to perform her redemptive mission, then God turned to Christianity, the younger, establishing with them a covenant of grace. This fact is implied in the author's expression "the time of reformation" in which the ministry of the earthly tabernacle gave way to that of the heavenly sanctuary. The word for reformation is one which comes from the verb meaning to set right or straight. It is a medical term used by Hippocrates for making straight misshapen limbs.

Dr. A. T. Robertson says that "Christianity itself is the great Reformation of the current Judaism (Pharisaism) and the spiritual Judaism foreshadowed by the old Abrahamic promise." In other words the promise given to Abraham had become misshapen through the failure of Judaism to live up to her covenant relation. In Christianity, therefore, Christ is the Great Physician who makes straight the misshapen limbs of his people as they progress toward the completion of God's redemptive purpose (cf. Heb. 12:12). This act Christ performs through his continuing ministry in the heavenly sanctuary (v. 12).

For Review and Further Study

1. What was the symbol of the old covenant? Name the two principal divisions of the tabernacle. What significance do we find in the articles placed within the ark?

2. Describe the ministry of the high priest on the Day of Atonement.

3. What is the heavenly sanctuary? Who is the High Priest of this sanctuary? What is meant by redemption?

4. What is the reformation?

7

WITHIN THE VEIL

[9:13 to 10:18]

WE NOW ENTER into the holy of holies of the epistle. All the foregoing evidence as to the superiority of Christianity over Judaism is preparatory to the solemn truth that the sacrifice of Christ is a better sacrifice (v. 23) than the multiple offerings made by a succession of priests of the line of Levi. Here we look into the very heart of God wherein we find indelibly inscribed the eternal purpose of God "which he purposed in Christ Jesus our Lord" (Eph. 3:11).

I. THE PERFECT NATURE OF THE SACRIFICE (vv. 13-14)

1. *The Imperfect Nature of Animal Sacrifice (v. 13)*

The sacrifices of Judaism were not without effect. Even so they had their limits. To this end the author directs our attention to two rituals of Old Testament sacrifice, both of which were significant with regard to the redemption and service of God's people.

We have seen already that the repetitious sacrifice of bulls and goats on the Day of Atonement served as a reminder of the continuing force of God's redemption of his people. Our author take cognizance of that fact (v. 13a) only to remind them that it was incomplete with regard to their day-to-day service for God. This fact emerges particularly in his reference to "the ashes of an heifer" (v. 13), which has to do with the rite prescribed by Jehovah for the cleansing of those who had become defiled by coming in contact with a dead person (Num. 19). Such a person was regarded as unclean for seven days and was, therefore, unfit for intercourse with God or man. Naturally he would be barred from any service for God or man. Remaining unclean beyond seven days, he was to be cut off from Israel, which implies his loss of the covenant relation.

For this rite of cleansing God prescribed that they should slay a red heifer which was without spot or blemish and which had never worn a yoke. Its body was to be burned, and the ashes, in turn, were to be mixed with water. Should a person touch a dead body, he was to be cleansed by having a clean person sprinkle him with this mixture on the third and seventh days.

Our author does not delve into the mystery of the cleansing power of blood, merely accepting it as a truth of divine revelation. But he reminds his readers that these two rites, while effective, were designed only to sanctify "to the purifying of the flesh" (v. 13). Being outward, they did not reach down into the inner nature of man (v. 9). The word "sanctify," according to Dr. Moffatt, means only that by this rite a man was restored to outward communion with God. However, we must not forget that the root meaning of that word implies the act of setting apart for God's service. Therefore we do not do violence to the text when we say that the author has in mind the fact that through the atoning sacrifice of bulls and goats, plus the cleansing rite of the ashes of an heifer, the recipient is made fit for God's use in his divine mission.

This thought is found everywhere throughout the epistle. Still we must remember that the "purifying of the flesh," apart from the inner nature, entails the limited nature of the old covenant in qualifying one for that service.

2. *The Efficacy of Christ's Sacrifice (v. 14a)*

However, if the blood of dumb animals could in God's power purify the flesh of man, how much more could the blood of Christ purge the inner nature of man, making him fit for God's service. This is true not only because his one sacrifice supersedes in effectiveness the many sacrifices of Judaism, but because of the nature of the sacrifice itself. In the former instance it was the unwilling sacrifice of unknowing victims. But in the case of Christ he offered himself "through the eternal Spirit," a spotless sacrifice. "Spirit" here does not refer to the Holy Spirit (10:15), but to the spirit of Christ. This involves not only his willingness, but more definitely it refers to the interplay of his personality upon the personality of man. His sacrifice was not outward and material but inward and spiritual. It was not a rite but a reality. Because Christ was what he was in his eternal nature, his blood could be effective for determining the absolute realities for man.

3. *The Result of Christ's Sacrifice (v. 14b)*

Whereas the blood of animals and the ashes of an heifer served to dedicate the Israelites to the purifying of the flesh, the blood of Christ purges man's "conscience from dead works to serve the living God." Conscience refers both to the forgiveness on the part of God and also to the consciousness of sins on the part of man.

The immediate idea in the mind of the author, however, is the contrast between *dead bodies* and *dead works.* Dr. Dods says that a pause might be put before works, "from dead—not bodies but—works." We may further compare "wicked works" (Col. 1:21) with "dead works" as used here. The suggestion is that wicked works are those deeds which are essentially wrong, while dead works may be good works which lack spiritual meaning and vitality. In any case, dead works are set over against dead bodies. As contact with a dead body made the Israelite unfit for fellowship and service with both God and man, so do dead works invalidate us in the same regard. Many Christian people are good, but they are good for nothing. They employ their time and energy in those things which are good within themselves but which lack spiritual meaning and vitality for the service of God to man.

But the blood of Christ is effective in purging us from these things, making us fit instruments in God's hands for our spiritual service. A redeemed man should see that the whole end of life for him is to be used of God for spiritual ends. If the good but meaningless activities of our everyday schedules usurp the place of allegiance in our lives, they become dead—and they cut us off from the onward sweep of God's purpose for his people. Only a renewal of our fellowship with Christ can purge us from such and prepare us for service to the living God.

II. The Purpose of the Sacrifice (vv. 15-28)

1. *The Promise of an Inheritance (v. 15)*

The background of the sacrificial system of Judaism was the covenant relation which God established with his people. We have seen that this relationship involved not only their redemption but also their part in God's plan for world redemption. In implementing this covenant, God has promised to them who were the "called" an inheritance involving both personal redemption and a life purpose. In addition, it pertained to the land of promise from which they were to operate in carrying out this purpose. Still further we have seen that this inheritance was transferred to *the called ones* who had avowed their allegiance to Christ. They had been redeemed and called by him for Christian growth and service. The efforts of our author are directed to leading this redeemed people into the state of mind and heart (their Canaan) from which they shall go on to the fulfilment of their divine destiny.

"For this cause" Jesus is the Mediator of the new covenant or testament that through his death he might validate the old and implement the new. The point which the author is making is simply that even the sacrifices of the old covenant which qualified the Israelites for divine service were meaningless apart from the ministry of Christ wherein he was both victim and High Priest. The only merit contained in the blood of bulls and goats and the ashes of an heifer was in the fact that they pointed forward to the redemptive work of Christ on Calvary and his continuing cleansing through his intercession at the right hand of God.

Dr. G. Campbell Morgan suggests this truth as the basis for the appearance with Jesus of Moses and Elijah on Mount Hermon. In effect they were saying to Jesus that if he stopped short of the cross, then all those who in the time past had believed in his coming sacrifice would be lost.

Thus it is clear that the sacrifice of Christ was not for the future only but for the whole of time. Before the world was created, he was the Lamb slain for the sins of the whole inhabited earth in every age. And as he calls men to salvation in every generation, so are the called to echo his word of invitation. This is the twofold inheritance of the people of God.

2. *The Provision for an Inheritance (vv. 16-24)*

To prove his point the author offers two illustrations, the one from secular law and the other from divine law. Any lawyer is happy when he can rely upon two such compelling arguments.

The example from secular law has to do with the making of a will. In verses 16-17 the word which is translated elsewhere in the epistle as *covenant* should here be rendered *testament* or will (cf. Gal. 3:15f.) A will, says he, is of no force (legal term) while the testator (legal term) lives; it is without strength (legal term) until the death of the testator is announced (legal term, almost in the sense of "proved"). When a man makes a will, he simply records his personal intention that after his death his beneficiaries shall receive a determined distribution of his estate. So long as he lives, it is simply a document which looks forward toward his death, but is invalid until that event can be proved to have taken place. No matter how much his beneficiaries may desire to receive the inheritance, they cannot do so until the testator dies. Ever after his death they can look back to that event as the thing which made effective the will of him who determined it to be so.

Implied in this citation is the thought that regardless of the intense desire on the part of the Old Testament worthies, their redemption was merely an expression of the will of God which could become their final possession only after the death of Christ. In short, they and all to whom they might minister would be saved *on credit* until the ransom was fully paid by the testator; a mixture of terms, to be sure, but the same idea.

Turning to divine law (vv. 18-23), the author reminds his readers that even the covenant of law was ratified by the death of a victim, the implication being that the victim stood in the place of the testator who is later identified as God in Christ. This reference is to Exodus 24 where Moses recorded the sealing of the covenant which God made with his people (Ex. 19:1-9). To do so, he took the blood of a sacrifice, placing half of it in a basin, and sprinkling the rest upon the altar. This latter act symbolized God's part in the covenant. Then he read the terms of the covenant to the people who accepted the covenant relation. After this he sprinkled the people with the remainder of the blood, thus symbolizing the sealing of the covenant on their behalf. Our author suggests that Moses also sprinkled the book of the covenant (v. 19). While this is not stated in Exodus, it is possible that it was done. Neither does Exodus mention the use of water, scarlet wool, and hyssop, although these were used in such rites. Dr. Moffatt notes that the author exercises "characteristic freedom" in the use of the Scriptures. Verse 20 contains the idea expressed by Moses (Ex. 24: 8), but the words are reminiscent of Jesus' words in Mark 14:24, which the author probably had in mind. It is a keen suggestion of the connection between the former event and the one to which he soon turns.

He closes this illustration by drawing the famous conclusion which has furnished the text for many sermons, "And almost all things [not all, but almost all, cf. Ex. 19:10; Lev. 5:11f.; and others] are by the law purged with blood; and without shedding of blood is no remission" (v. 22). The expression "shedding of blood" is a word coined by the writer meaning "pouring out of blood." Blood was considered as the principle of life (Lev. 17:11). In all ancient sacrificial religions when the victim poured out his blood, it poured out its life, said life believed to accrue to the benefit of the worshiper. God said, "It is the blood that maketh an atonement for the soul" (Lev. 17:11).

3. *The Proof of Our Inheritance (vv. 24-28)*

The author glides from the illustrations to their application, with a contrast between the cleansing of the earthly tabernacle, which was but a copy, and the heavenly sanctuary, which was the original (in eternity) and true tabernacle (v. 24). A matter of difficulty is seen by some in the latter part of this verse where it is inferred that heaven itself had to be purified. The problem dissolves when we recall that the writer is simply comparing the entrance of blood into the holy of holies with the appearance of the slain Christ within the heavenly veil. Actually the author applies his illustration rather freely, for his reference to Exodus 24 concerns an event which took place before the tabernacle was built (Ex. 25f.). Moses simply sprinkled the blood upon the altar which had been provided for the occasion, a practice which was later employed within the tabernacle. The altar signified the presence of God for redemption, whether in the tabernacle or outside it. The writer's mind is not bothered with minute details but with the tremendous thought which he now presents.

Whereas the old covenant or inheritance had been ratified with the blood of animals, the new covenant was validated by the blood of the Son of God. "For Christ is not entered into the holy places made with hands, which are the figures of the true; but into heaven itself, now to appear in the presence of God for us" (v. 24). This is an obvious comparison of Jesus' atoning work with that of the Levitical high priest. While blood is not specifically mentioned, it is implied (cf. 9:12).

The point of contrast is in the fact that while the Levitical high priest repeatedly entered into the holy place made with hands, bearing animal blood, Jesus entered into the heavenly holy of holies *once for all* (9:12) on our behalf. Under the old covenant the fellowship with God was repeatedly broken, and, therefore, the sacrifice had to be repeatedly made. The *once-for-all* sacrifice of Christ provides man with continuous access to God. One wonders how those who repeatedly *sacrifice* Christ in the Mass get around these verses!

In his atoning work Christ perfectly fulfilled every typical act of the high priest on the Day of Atonement. As the High Priest Jesus presented himself, pure in his own nature, before God. As the victim for the sacrifice he was without spot or blemish. As the high priest entered the holy place with the prayer of incense, so did Jesus pray to God for himself and for the people. In his death Jesus was our Scapegoat, bearing "our sins far away." As the high priest announced the atonement which was to be declared to all men, so did Jesus give his commission for world evangelism.

But the significant point in verses 24ff. is with regard to the entrance of the crucified Christ into heaven "to appear in the presence of God for us." Two words are worthy of careful notice. The first is "presence" whose root meaning in Greek is *face*. It further implies equality, being somewhat akin to the idea expressed in John 1:1, "face to face with God," or equal with God. This reference in John suggests the ancient Oriental custom of seating dignitaries of equal rank so that when they looked at one another, their faces or eyes met on an even line. When one was shorter than the other, pillows were placed beneath him to raise him to the level of the other so that the two could see "eye to eye."

The second word is "for" which is variously translated *in the place of* (John 11:50) or *on behalf of*. When one took the place of another, he was considered as standing or bending over the one whom he would shield or defend. When Jesus died, he did so in the place of man. Furthermore, after his resurrection he appeared face to face with the Father as an equal to bend over man to protect him from the anger of a righteous God against sin. Before a Christian can be lost again, the wages of sin must get by Jesus, which, of course, is impossible. Glorious is the gospel which has been given to us to preach to those over whom the wrath of God is poised!

We shall not delve into the mystery as to the exact time that Jesus appeared before God bearing in his person the blood of the sacrifice. It is an intriguing thought! The important thing is that he did appear—and is still there—as an equal before God, bending over us to shield us as he ever holds intercession for us. Intercession here is not to be interpreted as the act of an inferior being begging a favor from one who is superior. Rather it involves the idea of an equal claiming that which is due on the basis of the evidence presented. In intercession Jesus stands before God as an equal, claiming the souls of men on the basis of his sacrifice for sin and his victory over the power of sin and death.

The glorious truth is that Jesus appeared in the fulness of time (Gal. 4:4; cf. Heb. 9:26, "in the end of the world") "to put away sin by the sacrifice of himself" (v. 26). He dealt with sin as a principle, not with individual sins as did the Levitical system (Robertson). And as man must die once to appear before God in judgment (v. 27), so did Christ appear the first time to die *once for all* to bear the sin of the many who believe on him; that when they appear for judgment, they shall find that they have already been judged in Christ, who shall appear the second time apart from sin unto the full salvation toward which we move (v. 28). In the meantime we must not, like the Hebrew Christians, despair of the second coming of Christ, but must in that blessed hope continue about the Father's business, for he is the proof of our inheritance.

III. The Persons of the Sacrifice (10:1-18)

The author is rapidly coming to the end of his argument. All that precedes and follows 9:13 to 10:18 is based upon the fact that in Christ we have a better sacrifice than that of Judaism. Hebrews 10:1-4 is a summary of this whole matter. Why was it necessary that the Son of God should die? The answer is found in the incompleteness of the Levitical sacrifices. They were of law rather than of grace (v. 1). Being imperfect, they must be repeated (vv. 1-2). Because their victims were nonmoral, they were outward and material rather than inward and spiritual (v. 2). Instead of ending man's consciousness of sin, they were a constant reminder of sin (vv. 2-3). Bereft of personality themselves these sacrifices were impotent in reaching the personality of man to cleanse him from sin (v. 4). To accomplish the whole purpose of God in redemption, there must be an interplay of persons which involved the whole of God for all of man. When all else had failed, God supplied the need. Thus we see the triune God engaging all his power in one great act of redemption. This engagement is seen in the will of God, the work of Christ, and the witness of the Holy Spirit.

1. *The Will of the Father (vv. 5-7)*

The will of God in redemption is evident throughout the Scriptures. Elsewhere we have noted that God was determined to renew the broken fellowship for which man was made. In every promise from Genesis 3:15 onward, the scarlet thread of redemption permeates the revelation of God. He knew from the beginning that man would sin. An omniscient God was aware of the inability of man ever accomplishing redemption for himself either through personal endeavor or through a prescribed system of laws and sacrificial rites. But despite that knowledge on the part of God, it was not yet evident to man. For that reason man, in order to be willing for the fellowship to be renewed, must be given his opportunity only to fail. Until that time man would be incapable of forsaking everything else to turn in repentance

and faith to God himself. Only in that manner would
man fully admit his guilt and throw himself upon the
mercy of God. Until that happened, the broken fellowship could not be restored.

Knowing from before the foundation of the world that
he could have no pleasure in burnt offerings and sacrifices for sin (v. 6), God's will (v. 7) led him to prepare
against that day when man would forsake self-reliance to
turn to the living God. Aware that he ultimately must
become both *just* and the *Justifier,* he prepared for the
incarnation of God (v. 5) that he might take upon himself the infirmities of men. This purpose was recorded in
the Book of revelation (v. 7) that man might look forward in faith and hope, and that he might recognize the
event when it happened in the incarnation of the Son
of God (John 1:11, 14).

2. *The Work of the Son (vv. 8-14)*

The will of God involved also the will of the Son.
Since he was to be the victim of the sacrifice, there must
be a willingness on his part. Otherwise he would have
been only one of a multitude of unwilling victims. But
the glorious truth is that he did say to his Father, in
eternity as well as in time, "Not what I will, but what
thou wilt" (Mark 14:36). The author points out this fact
by quoting from Psalm 40, "When he said, Sacrifice and
offering and burnt offerings and offering for sin thou
wouldst not, neither hadst pleasure therein; which are
offered by the law; then said he, Lo, I come to do thy will,
O God" (vv. 8-9). This quotation, according to Dr. A. T.
Robertson, includes the whole body of Old Testament
sacrifice: animal offering, the meal offering, the burnt
offering, and the sin offering. When it was evident that
all or none of these could suffice, the Son willingly offered
himself, that "through the offering of the body of Jesus

Christ [his human-divine nature] once for all" (v. 10) those who would believe in him might be sanctified. Thus they would be purified (redeemed) and dedicated as fit vessels of God's mercy to all men.

The efficacy of his sacrifice is seen in the fact that in contrast to the continual sacrifices of the Levitical high priest, "this man, after he had offered one sacrifice for sins for ever, sat down on the right hand of God" (v. 12). There was no seat in the holy of holies, because the work of Aaron was never finished. But after Jesus cried, "It is finished" (John 19:30), he sat down, for his work was complete, never again to be repeated. The word *is finished* is the perfect tense of the word meaning to reach a desired and purposeful end. The perfect tense expresses the idea that a thing happened in the past, is still going on, and shall continue to go on. Thus Christ's redemptive work avails for past, present, and future. Paul used the same perfect tense (passive) in Ephesians 2:8 where he said, "For by grace are ye saved." As the result of our Lord's finished work, those who believed in him were saved when they believed, they are saved, and will continue to be saved forever (cf. John 5: 24).

It is of interest to note further that Jesus sat down on the *right hand of God.* That was the position of power. Because of his sacrifice he is both willing and mighty to save.

We cannot pass by this section without noting another matter of interest to the Christian. Here Jesus is seen as sitting down after the ascension. But when Stephen, the first martyr, was dying he saw Jesus "standing on the right hand of God" (Acts 7:56). This is significant. Here was the first Christian who was called upon to prove his faithfulness unto the point of dying (cf. Rev. 2:10). Upon his faith rested in a measure the future of the cause of Christ. If he failed, others would fail, and, perhaps, the cause with them. If he persisted, others would do likewise, and the cause would be safe. So interested was Jesus in this duel to the death between the faith of Stephen and those who were determined to blot out the very name of Jesus, that he stood up.

This is not fanciful reasoning, but a truth of Christian history. Jesus suffers with his people. When they are persecuted, he is persecuted (Acts 9:4). As their High Priest he sustains them so that even the blood of his martyrs becomes the seed of his church. This is a fact pregnant with meaning both for those who first read this epistle and for those of us who study it now.

What is Jesus doing now as he sits on the right hand of God? Elsewhere we see Jesus *face to face* with God, as our substitute in sacrifice (9:24), and as the one who is touched with the feeling of our infirmities (4:15), holding intercession for us (7:25). These are continuous offices of our High Priest. But here we see him as our King *seated alongside* God in the position of power— "from henceforth expecting till his enemies be made his footstool" (v. 13). Such a result had been promised to him as the fruit of his sacrifice (1:8-13). Now, having finished his work, he is expecting. Such an attitude of expectancy would imply that the full realization of the promise is yet in the future.

Who are the enemies to which reference is made? Paul speaks of the time when Christ shall "put down all rule and all authority and power. For he must reign, till he hath put all enemies under his feet. The last enemy that shall be destroyed is death" (1 Cor. 15: 24-26). His primary thought there being the resurrection, naturally he points out death. But he also infers other enemies as typified by *rule, authority,* and *power.* These are elsewhere designated by him as *principalities, powers, rulers of the darkness of this world,* and *spiritual wickedness in heavenly places* (Eph. 6:12). Therefore the enemies mentioned there and in our epistle obviously refer to the forces of evil as embodied in the prince of this world (John 12:31). In John the prince of this world is said to have been cast out through the crucifixion of Jesus (cf. 1 John 3:8). Thus the power of the evil one as manifested both in the natural order and in the human family is ultimately to be destroyed by the power of the crucified and living Christ. In the realm of the human family this victory waits upon the obedience of those who have been redeemed into the new covenant relationship. While we delay, still our Lord waits— *expecting.*

3. *The Witness of the Holy Spirit (vv. 15-18)*

The expectant attitude of the Son is augmented by the witness of the Holy Spirit. Thus we see that the triune God is engaged in the plan of redemption. It is not necessary that we look into the mystery of the Trinity in its essential nature or its practical application here. Needless time might be consumed in debating the question as to how God could satisfy his holiness through his own death, or as to the necessity of God interceding with himself. We have seen that this implies not the act of begging for a favor, but the continuous evidence of the atonement and its merit. It is sufficient merely to remember that world redemption employs the whole of God's nature. God the Father proposed it; God the Son provided it; God the Holy Spirit propagates it.

The point of emphasis here is the specific work of the Holy Spirit in redemption. The primary thought of the author is the work of the Holy Spirit in revelation whereby he has revealed the redemptive will of God and its accomplishment in the Son. He is the source of the word about the new covenant which has been made effective by the Son (vv. 17-18). This the Holy Spirit has revealed "to us"—to us Christians.

However, we cannot ignore in this connection the over-all work of the Holy Spirit in a full and complete salvation. He is the one who convicts the world with respect to sin, righteousness, and judgment (John 16:8ff.). He is the Agent of the new birth (John 3:5). Furthermore, we have his witness in our hearts that we are children of God (1 John 5:7ff.).

If we are correct in our position as to the general thesis of the epistle, the author may well have had in mind also the perfecting of our salvation. He is our Comforter in sorrow, our Counselor in our growth in grace and knowledge of Christ, and our Companion in Christian service. He makes dynamic our witness as he guides us in doing the full will of God. The Holy Spirit animates, empowers, and directs the redeemed toward the realization of God's will and Christ's work.

This is a precious truth to us as it was to the Hebrew Christians. Beset on every hand by trials and temptations as we are, yet we are not alone. The One who in his one offering perfected us, or fitted us for a desired purpose, and sanctified us, or set us apart to the service of God (v. 14), is through the Holy Spirit our Partner in our enlarged, ever-beckoning task.

The author concludes the argument of the entire epistle thus far by reminding his readers of the important part which they must play in this endeavor: "Now where remission of these [sins and iniquities] is, there is no more offering for sin" (v. 18). Just as there is no more offering for their personal redemption, so is there no further offering for the sin of the whole world. We must not wait for some other sacrificial act of God in world redemption. *God has finished his part. The rest waits upon us!*

For Review and Further Study

1. What was the significance of "the ashes of an heifer"? How was the sacrifice of Christ superior to animal sacrifice? Distinguish between "dead works" and "wicked works."

2. How were people saved before Calvary? What was necessary to put a will or testament into effect? What is the proof of our inheritance? Is Christ equal with God? What is meant by the intercession of Jesus before God?

3. Who willed the redemption of man? Who provided the redemption of man? Who propagates this redemption? What is Jesus doing as he is seated at the right hand of God?

8

CLAIMING THE PROMISE

[6:13-14; 8:6; 10:19 to 11:40]

Having completed the argument of the epistle, our author now proceeds to apply its truth to the practical aspects of Christian living. It is not enough to have a greater High Priest who saves to the uttermost. Spiritual possession cannot be said to be real until it evolves itself into a better manner of life. Grace to be appropriated must be shared. With that in mind we are brought face to face with the fact that under the new and better covenant we have a better promise as to its relationship to the immediate problem at hand—that of transforming principle into performance.

I. The Promise of the Covenant (6:13-14; 8:6; 10:23)

1. *The Promise Made to Abraham's Seed (6:13-14; cf. Gen. 12:1-3)*

The basic covenant upon which the theme of the epistle rests is the one which God made with Abraham (Gen. 12:1-3; cf. Heb. 6:13f.). This is the definite beginning of the implementing of God's plan of redemption. Heretofore God's covenants with Adam and Noah had been of a general nature. But when we come to Abraham, we find that God has chosen a line through which his redemptive purpose is to run. The future covenants are but outgrowths of this purpose.

In making this covenant, God gave to Abraham and his seed a definite promise conditioned upon their acceptance of a particular responsibility: "And I will make of thee a great nation, and I will bless thee, and make thy name great; and thou shalt be a blessing" (Gen. 12:2). Here God made a threefold promise. He will make of Abraham's seed a great nation; he will bless that nation; he will make its name great. All these things God swore by himself to perform (Heb. 6:13f.). But to that promise God attached a condition—"and thou shalt be a blessing." Our author quotes only the promise, but he implies the condition when he says that after Abraham had patiently endured, he obtained the promise (6:15). In other words, the promise here was made operative only through the obedience of the patriarch in fulfilling the condition.

We remind ourselves once more that the failure of Israel was not due to the inability or unwillingness of God to keep his promise. It was due always to her failure to fulfil the condition. God stood ever ready to provide in proportion to Israel's readiness to appropriate. When it became evident that she would not use her covenant relation to its designed end, God disannulled it in that he provided a new covenant for a new people. In her rebellion against the will of God, Israel lost the promise.

2. *The Promise Made to Christ's Seed (8:6)*

The covenant mentioned by Jeremiah became operative with the appearance of Christ in history. He was the Mediator of this better covenant which rested upon better promises (8:6). As God sent him into the world, so did he send his *seed* into the world (John 20:21). They were not promised immunity from trials (John 15:18ff.), but were assured that he would be with them through them (Matt. 28:19f.). This is equivalent to the promise to Abraham that God would bless those who blessed his people and would curse those who cursed them—to the end that in them the whole world would be blessed (Gen.

12:3). Those who blessed or cursed the people of God did so to God himself. Hence God was identified with his people (cf. Acts 9:4).

The promise of Christ's abiding presence was fulfilled with the coming of the Holy Spirit (John 14:16). Thus we see the better promise of the new covenant. As God promised his presence with Israel in carrying out her mission, so did Christ promise his presence to Christians. But it was a better promise inasmuch as God's presence was typified by the tabernacle, whereas Christ's presence was realized in the personal presence of God in the Spirit. Whithersoever the Israelites went they had to *take* their symbol of God's presence with them; but under the covenant written upon the heart the Christian people have the Presence within. To this end, therefore, they have also the greater responsibility even as God himself is greater than his tabernacle. Only in the keeping of their obligation can they be said to have the promise.

This responsibility is seen further in the fact that under the new covenant God's people have more to offer. This thought is involved in the better promises. Whereas under the old covenant Israel could promise only a redemption to be realized by a future act of God, the Christian people have a complete gospel to proclaim. In Christ God has not only said his last word to man; he has also performed his last act for the redemption of man. Naturally, therefore, the Christian has the greater responsibility in making known this fact to a lost world.

3. *The Faithfulness of Him Who Promised (10:23)*

The promise made to Abraham rested upon the fidelity of the two parties to the covenant. If one kept his bargain, the other was obligated to do likewise. God's promise was on deposit and available whenever and wherever needed. Therefore the first act of good faith must be on the part of the party of the second part. Until that happened, the party of the first part had no responsibility. When Abraham was obedient, God was faithful. Israel sometimes questioned God when the problem lay within herself.

God is ready and faithful to fulfil his promise, but his people must show good faith that they are working at the job. God does not present us with full payment in advance, but he gives strength for each trial and each task. "The Lord is not slack concerning his promise" (2 Peter 3:9). If we fail to receive it, the failure is our own.

II. THE CONDITIONAL NATURE OF THE BETTER PROMISE (10:19-39)

The same condition applies to the new covenant as to the old. There is both a divine and a human side to the agreement. Thus far in the epistle we see that God has kept his bargain to make available the promise; the completed work awaits the compliance of his people.

1. *The Divine Condition for the Promise (vv. 19-21)*

The divine condition in the new covenant as in the old was the promise of the presence of God and all that his presence entailed. Under the old covenant that presence was symbolized in the tabernacle and particularly in the holy of holies. However, we have noted the limited aspect of it in that the priests alone could minister in the tabernacle, and only the high priest could enter the holy place once each year. Even so, the people were to stand off from the tabernacle, suggesting that even then God was not approachable except through another (Num. 18:22).

But through the Mediator of the new covenant, God's

presence is personal and unlimited to those who come to him through Christ. This fact is introduced by the author when he says "Having therefore, brethren, boldness to enter into the holiest by the blood of Jesus. . ." (v. 19). "Therefore" reverts back to the evidence just produced as to the sacrificial and intercessory ministry of Jesus Christ. The word "having" is a present participle which implies the continuing nature of the Christian's possession. He has it for the present as well as for the future. "Boldness" is likewise rendered *liberty;* which expresses the nature of the privilege. This liberty is given by the blood of Jesus. The way into the holy of holies is a "new and living way," *new* having the idea of *freshness.* Thus the sacrifice of Jesus is forever regarded as having just been made. It shall never lose its power.

This reference (v. 20) has to do with the veil which separated the holy of holies from the outer tabernacle. The author infers that the veil here means the flesh of Jesus. Some see in this the thought that in his flesh Jesus obscured the deity of Christ, while others see in it the revelation of God in the human body of Christ (John 1:18; 14:9). But the natural idea seems to be to connect it with the actual temple veil. When Jesus died, Matthew tells us that the veil "was rent in twain from the top to the bottom" (Matt. 27:51). This was accomplished by the death of Jesus, who was the Word made flesh (John 1:14). However we take it, the thought is clear that in Jesus, who is God manifested in the flesh, we have access to God. The separating veil has forever been removed by the blood of Jesus.

Jesus has entered into the veil of heaven itself as evidence before God of our redemption, and to remain forever as our High Priest, holding intercession for us throughout our continuing earthly trials. For this reason, we have the assurance of our own entrance into heaven.

However, we must not lose sight of the particular meaning at this point. The thought of the author is not only of our ultimate salvation but of our present responsibility. The covenant includes both. Therefore our *liberty* to approach God is a guarantee of his continuing presence with his people as they pursue their earthly destiny as well as their heavenly goal. Truly the divine condition of the promise has been met.

2. *The Human Condition for the Promise (vv. 22-25)*

But it is not yet clear that the Hebrew Christians have met their part of the covenant. Its operation depends upon their faithfulness to a task. For that reason the author gives to them a threefold exhortation to faithfulness.

"Let us draw near" (v. 22). Because Christ has given access to the presence of God, they are to avail themselves of it. They are to do so with a true heart or with loyalty to their calling. They are to do so in full assurance that his presence shall be realized. This is possible because Christ has cleansed their inner natures by his blood, and their bodies have been washed with pure water. This latter reference does not mean Christian baptism, but the act of ablution on the part of the high priest in connection with the sacrifice. Dr. Moffatt notes that in ancient thought the *heart* and the *body* are "a full plastic expression for the entire personality." In Christ they are wholly clean, which gives them the liberty to enjoy the presence of God.

"Let us hold fast" (v. 23). They are to retain their profession without wavering. That profession is the acceptance of their part of the new covenant. They are to *stick to the job,* knowing that God is faithful to keep his promise if they keep theirs.

"Let us consider one another" (v. 24). Already they

have been urged to consider Jesus (3:1). Now they are
to consider one another. The verb means to *fix one's
eye or mind* on one another. They are to keep an eye on
one another to watch for any tendency toward failure.
This is a duty enjoined upon all Christians to watch over
one another in brotherly love. In so doing we provoke
one another to love and to good works. This is to be
done in faith, hope, and love, the three Christian graces
which are expressed in the three exhortations—*faith* in
the efficacy of Christ (v. 22), *hope* in the faithfulness of
God (v. 23), and *love* for the brethren who have been
hallowed by the Holy Spirit (v. 24).

To do this they are to strengthen one another in
public worship and unified service, both of which are
involved in the assembling of themselves together. Some
of them already have been weakened by the neglect of
their assembling together. The program of Christ is not
an isolated matter but a communion of service. Christian
people do better that which they do together, whether
it be mystical communion with God or practical service
to man. Christians, like coals of fire, cease to glow when
they become separated from the group. God has promised
not to forsake them (v. 23). Thus they are to exhort one
another to faithfulness all the more because they see "the
day approaching." This may refer either to the second
coming of Christ which is ever imminent, or it may be a
reference to the coming destruction of Jerusalem. In
either case it involved a cataclysmic development in the
progress of the kingdom, making it all the more important that they be found faithful to their task.

3. The Consequence of Rejecting the Human Condi-
tion (vv. 26-31)

Failure to *stick to the job* is not without direful consequence. In introducing this thought the author leads

us to another of his exhortations which involve incalculable difficulties in interpretation.

In verse 26 he says that for those who keep on sinning (present participle) wilfully after having received a full knowledge of the truth, there remains no more sacrifice for sins. As in 6:4f. it appears that he is speaking of those who have had a genuine experience of grace, but who continue to sin repeatedly and wilfully. It is important to note that the sin referred to here is the sin of *standing off from* God (6:6) as he seeks to lead them on in Christian development for service. As elsewhere we take it that there is no evidence of apostasy in the usual sense of that word. He further says that for such there remains no more sacrifice for *sins* (plural). Man is redeemed from *sin,* not *sins.* Israel received a corresponding redemption from Egyptian bondage. But the tabernacle sacrifices were for the purpose of removing sins which made the people unfit for divine fellowship in service. Jesus redeemed his people from *sin* in his once-for-all sacrifice (1 John 1:7), a sacrifice which evolved into his ministry within the veil designed to free them from the *sins* which violate their fellowship for service with God (1 John 2:1). Reflecting back again, we recall that Israel's sins finally brought about her wilful sin of provocation at Kadesh-barnea. After that there was no more sacrifice which could restore that generation to the divine mission. In like manner, if Christian people in any generation provoke God in sinning wilfully against their spiritual destiny, they, too, shall be cut off from the redemptive purpose of God.

Instead they shall look only for "judgment and fiery indignation" (v. 27). Reference here is sometimes made to 2 Thessalonians 1:8-10, but an examination will show that Paul has in mind the fate of the unredeemed, while our author is apparently speaking of a redeemed people.

They shall not be lost, but they shall experience *divine anger marked by fire* (Robertson).

In support of this statement the author refers them to the law under the old covenant whereby those who despised the covenant relation should die at the mouth of two or three witnesses (v. 28; cf. Deut. 17:1-7). In Deuteronomy the specific case involves one who has gone off after the idolatrous worship of the sun, moon, or the hosts of heaven. This has even led some to suppose that the Hebrew Christians were guilty of such. We should remember, however, that the statement begins with a reference to those who *transgress the covenant with God*. This is the focal point in our author's mind, not the detailed sins by which the covenant was despised. Such sin certainly will make the sinner useless in evangelizing the pagan whose sins he had adopted.

Using the argument from the lesser to the greater, our author applies his illustration to his readers. If under the old covenant one who transgressed that relation should die, how much more will it apply under the new covenant: "Of how much sorer punishment, suppose ye, shall he be thought worthy, who hath trodden under foot the Son of God, and hath counted the blood of the covenant, wherewith he was sanctified, an unholy thing, and hath done despite unto the Spirit of grace?" (v. 29).

Following the line in those passages in which the author refers to apostasy, most scholars take this passage to mean that here. But we have pointed out elsewhere that the supposed references to apostasy probably have to do not with the act of forsaking God to go back into an unredeemed state, but with a refusal to go on in the covenant relation toward Christian growth and service. We believe that the same idea holds here. The context which colors the interpretation of our particular passage supports this contention. Furthermore, such a position does not strain the meaning of the ideas contained in it. In turning from their spiritual destiny, the Hebrew Christians do tread in contempt upon the Son of God as the Saviour of the whole world. They identify themselves with the crucifiers in setting at naught the redemptive mission of the Son of God (6:6). They thus count the blood which sealed their redemption and sanctified them for a task as unholy in that they refuse to share their experience with others. Furthermore, they do despite to or insult the Spirit of grace, who was given to be their dynamic partner in this service.

These are terrible pictures of the attitude of those who receive the blessing of salvation, but who negate its wider effect by refusing to share it with others. For such, a fate worse than physical death is in store. They shall perish in the wilderness of a lost opportunity. The world is full of such Christians today.

The certainty of their punishment is shown by two quotations from Deuteronomy 32:35f. (v. 30). "Vengeance belongeth unto me, I will recompense, saith the Lord. And again, The Lord shall judge his people." These utterances came at the climax of Moses' last words to Israel. He began by calling heaven and earth to witness to God's redemptive purpose: "My doctrine shall drop as the rain, my speech shall distil as the dew, as the small rain upon the tender herb, and as the showers upon the grass: because I will publish the name of the Lord: ascribe ye greatness unto our God" (Deut. 32:2-3). He then proceeds to show how God prepared a people for this purpose (32:7-14), only to have them rebel (32:15ff.). As a result they shall suffer punishment at the hands of another nation. In the end, however, he will avenge his people (32:35f.). In conclusion Moses exhorted the Israelites to remember these words and to tell them to their children. "For it is not a vain thing for you [to disregard

your covenant relation]; *because it is your life* [author's
italics]: and through this thing ye shall prolong your days
in the land, whither ye go over Jordan to possess it"
(32:47).

Instead of making our author take the quotations of
Deuteronomy 32:35f. out of their context and do violence
to their meaning in applying them to the people of God
rather than to their enemies, as some scholars do, may
we not naturally regard them as a reminder to his readers
of the entire passage in Deuteronomy with which they
most certainly were familiar? If so, they carry even more
force as a warning to them. Even though God will ultimately avenge his people by honoring his own part of
the covenant relation whereby they are declared to be
his people, the suffering which they endure because of
their unfaithfulness in that regard is horrible beyond
expression. It is indeed "a fearful thing to fall into the
hands of the living God" (v. 31) who will not take lightly
their own denial of the covenant which they have made
with him.

4. *The Partial Fulfilment of Their Condition (vv. 32-39)*

That the author has the entire passage in Deuteronomy
32 in mind is seen further as he proceeds to exhort the
people to faithfulness. In the aforementioned passage
Moses said, "Remember the days of old . . ." (32:7) how
God had provided for them and protected them in trials
in order to prepare them for their mission. From this
point of departure our author says, "But call to remem-
brance the former days, . . . (vv. 32ff.), that after they
were illuminated or saved, God kept them through a
great trial of afflictions. In enduring such trials they had
begun to realize their destiny. Now, he says, do not cast
away as worthless the boldness which you thus gained

(v. 35). As God kept them through past trials, he will preserve them in the future. So long as they go on in their Christian development and service, God will be faithful to his promise.

To do so they will need patience (v. 36). Unfortunately we read into that word our modern meaning of passive endurance. The Greek word used here is a red-blooded word. In the papyri it is used as the term for a military decoration given for heroism in battle. A *patient* soldier was one who could take all that the enemy could send against him and give back a little more in return. In their trials, therefore, these Hebrew Christians are to endure all that their persecutors can give, and then have enough reserve to countercharge to victory. In so doing, they shall receive the promise (v. 36). Furthermore, though they despair of the Lord's return, he will surely return to reward them for their faithfulness (v. 37). This is the blessed hope of every Christian!

In concluding this exhortation to faithful endurance, the author quotes from Habakkuk 2:4, "The just shall live by faith." This is the only verse from the Old Testament which is quoted three times in the New Testament (Rom. 1:17; Gal. 3:11; Heb. 10:38). "But," says he, "if any man draw back, my soul shall have no pleasure in him" (v. 38). The word *draw back* or shrink back carries the idea of fear which makes one withdraw from his duty. In such God has no delight.

However, he reminds them of his confidence in them as being those who do not shrink back unto destruction (v. 39). The word translated *perdition* carries here not so much the modern idea of hell as that of destruction, which was the fate of the Israelites who shrank back in fear from their duty at Kadesh-barnea. Instead, the author is convinced that his readers are those who shall prove faithful unto the full salvation of their lives (v. 39).

The word here translated *soul* in classical Greek and in Philo is sometimes used for *life*. In both, the exact phrase here is used as the equivalent of saving one's life. That is most probably the meaning here. Thus in shrinking back in unbelief their lives would be destroyed, but in pursuing their divine destiny through faith in him that promised their lives will be saved.

III. THE BASIS FOR RECEIVING THE PROMISE (11:1-40)

Since faith is the deciding element in receiving the promise of our covenant, it is essential that we understand what faith is and how it works. Therefore our author concludes this phase of his exhortation by citing the record of the faithful throughout their past history.

1. *The Essence of Faith (v. 1)*

"Now faith is the substance of things hoped for, the evidence of things not seen." Thus we are reminded that faith is not some idealistic and idle experience; it is the very undergirding substance of life. The word "substance" is from the word used by Aristotle and others to refer to that which stands under anything, such as a building, a contract, or a promise. It is often found in the papyri in business documents as the basis or guarantee of transactions. We may best translate it here as the *title-deed* of things hoped for. Furthermore, the word "evidence" is from an old Greek word meaning *proof* or *conviction*. Faith then is the title-deed of things which have been promised and the *proof* of the reality of the invisible.

It is on this basis that faith becomes operative in life as we look beyond conditions as they are to that which they may become. When Christian people are tempted to magnify their present difficulties in the face of their destiny, they will do well to look beyond them to the promise and power of God in the accomplishing of his purpose.

2. *The Example of the Faithful Under the Old Covenant (vv. 2-38)*

That faith is the title-deed and proof of the reality of the invisible is seen in the experiences of those who have put it to the test in the crucible of actual experience. The spiritual forebears (v. 2) of the Hebrew Christians had proved their faith only to find that he was faithful who had promised (10:23).

For convenience we may divide the list of the heroes of faith into those from Adam to Abraham (vv. 3-7); from Abraham through Joshua (vv. 8-31); and from the period of the Judges to the time of Christ (vv. 32-38).

By faith, therefore, we understand that the ages were made by the spoken word of God (Gen. 1:1), so that the visible universe was made out of invisible things. There is a hint of the findings of modern science wherein visible matter is understood to be composed of invisible atoms. Likewise, we see by suggestion that even in material things there is a reality of the invisible.

Passing from inanimate nature to the realm of the personal, we are told that by the same kind of faith Abel was declared righteous by his obedience to God's prescribed method of sacrifice (v. 4; cf. Gen. 4:4). And although he has been dead for milleniums, his faith still testifies to such. By faith Enoch was translated, his tombless and timeless epitaph being that by his faith he had pleased (perfect tense) God (v. 5; cf. Gen. 5:24). Such faithfulness to God is that which is born of a conviction that God lives and rewards those who seek after him (v. 6). By faith Noah looked more than a century into the future to see the reality of God's warning. He believed God's message about the flood. And despite the jeers of men, he prepared an ark unto the saving of the life of his entire household (v. 7; cf. Gen. 6-9). In so doing he condemned an unbelieving world and became heir to the righteousness which is by faith.

From these brief mentions of faith the author passes to the extended example of the father of the faithful, Abraham. While in the foregoing instances the redemptive purpose of God is seen only by implication, in this passage the relation of faith to the eternal purpose of God becomes clear. It was an act of explicit faith which led Abraham to leave the seemingly sure foundation of an orderly life to journey into the unknown in response to the promise of God that he would receive the Land of Promise as an inheritance (Gen. 12:1-5). He did not even know where the land was, yet he went. In the land which was promised to him he lived out his life, as did his son and grandson, as a nomadic stranger. But though they dwelt in tents whose only foundation were pegs driven into the sand, despite disappointment they wavered not since they looked for "a city which hath foundations, whose builder and maker is God" (vv. 8-11).

A still greater trial of the faith of Abraham, and Sarah, was in regard to the birth of an heir of the promise (vv. 11-12; cf. Gen. 15:1-5). Though both were far beyond the age of childbearing, yet by faith they realized the faithfulness of him who promised. Powerless within themselves to conceive, by their faith they were made fertile. True their faith did waver for a time (Gen. 16), yet by faith they overcame and went on to receive the promise. Although they died without receiving the full realization of God's promise, yet they died believing that it yet would be. Abraham did in joy receive the promise of the Messiah (John 8:56), yet he greeted it as afar off (v. 13), not living to see his actual appearance to seal the promise of world redemption. Because of their will to believe in him who had promised they did not, like the Israelites at Kadesh-barnea, turn back. God, in turn, was not ashamed to be called their God (vv. 13-16).

But the supreme test of Abraham's faith came when God told him to sacrifice Isaac, his son of the promise (Gen. 22; 17:1a). The test involved not merely a father's love for his son, but the patriarch's faith in God and his redemptive purpose. For Isaac was not just a son; he was the miracle-born son through whom God's redemptive line was to proceed. To slay him apparently would write *finis* to the promise.

The similarity between the near death of Isaac, Abraham's only begotten son (v. 17), and Jesus, God's only begotten Son, cannot be overlooked. In both instances, the natural supposition would be that the event would mark the defeat of God's purpose. But, unlike the crucifiers, Abraham acted in faith that even then God would raise up the heir of promise (v. 19). In so doing he also prefigured faith in the resurrection of Jesus. The faith that was in Abraham's heart persisted in the person of his son, Isaac; his grandson, Jacob; and his great-grandson, Joseph (vv. 20-22). Despite seeming delay in the fulfilment of the purpose, they still believed in the faithfulness of him who promised. In short, their faith was grounded not in the visible but in the invisible.

The example of the author is a progressive one. Turning, therefore, from the earlier patriarchs he cites the faithfulness of Moses in all his house (3:2). Even in the infancy of Moses the faith of his parents served to preserve him for his place in God's redemptive mission (v. 23). And that same faith was found in Moses, who, when as a grown man who could make his own choices, refused a place of luxury "choosing rather to suffer affliction with the people of God, than to enjoy the pleasures of sin for a season" (v. 25). This was a delib-

erate choice, for he regarded the reproach of being a
follower of Christ as greater riches than the material
riches of Egypt. The author says that in his choice Moses
"kept on looking away" (Robertson) from the riches of
Egypt unto the reward which would be his in faithfully
following Christ (v. 26). That his choice was not only
a measure of values but an act of boldness is seen in the
fact that he forsook Egypt, not from fear of Pharoah,
but because he saw him who was invisible. Before the
incident which precipitated his flight from Egypt, Moses
had already made his choice (Ex. 2:11-15). His continuing faith in the redemptive purpose of God is seen
in that he instituted the Passover at the word of God,
whereby the first-born of Israel was saved (v. 28).

To the author the climax of Moses' faith is regarded
as his act in leading the children of Israel out of Egypt
through the Red Sea (v. 29; cf. Ex. 14). He sees in this
not only the faith of Moses but that of his people in
contrast to the unbelieving Egyptians. Implied throughout these examples is the thought that as God's people
of old succeeded by faith, so would the Hebrew Christians
likewise succeed or fail according to their faith.

Furthermore, it was by faith that the children of
Israel under Joshua finally received the promise given
to Abraham. Apart from their faith the mighty victory
at Jericho would have been a military monstrosity. It
would seem that the author's reference to the faith of
Rahab is to point out the working of faith even through
the most unlikely people (v. 31). But even in the case
of one who was not a racial descendant of Abraham, her
faith in the reality of the invisible sufficed to achieve
the purpose of God.

From this point the author despairs of time or space
in which to summon up his great "cloud of witnesses."
He must be content to summarize their exploits of faith.

Even so we can with a fair degree of accuracy identify them. Mentioning a few by name (v. 32), he plunges into a bare reference to their mighty deeds (vv. 33-35). In faith they subdued kingdoms (cf. Judg. 4:6ff.; 6:11ff.; 11:1ff; 13:24ff.; 2 Sam. 5:ff.), wrought righteousness (Acts 10:35), obtained promises (2 Sam. 7:11), stopped the mouths of lions (Dan. 6:18ff.), quenched the violence of fire (Dan. 3:19ff.), escaped the edge of the sword (1 Sam. 18:11; 1 Kings 19:2), out of weakness were made strong (Judg. 16:26ff.), waxed valiant in fight (Psalm 18:34ff.), turned to flight the armies of aliens (Judg. 7:21), and women received their dead raised to life again (1 Kings 17:17ff.; 2 Kings 4:8ff.). They were stoned to death (1 Kings 21:13), sawn asunder (the traditional death of Isaiah), slain with the sword (Jer. 26:23), wandered about in sheepskins and goatskins (2 Kings 1:8), being destitute, afflicted, and tormented (v. 37).

In addition to his list of canonical heroes, the author cites two examples from the history of the interbiblical trials of God's people: "others were tortured, not accepting deliverance; that they might obtain a better resurrection" (v. 35). The reference no doubt is to an incident recorded in an Apocryphal book, 2 Maccabees 7. Antiochus Epiphanes of Syria had set himself to a program designed to break the tenacious resistance of the Jews by introducing among them Greek culture and religion. On a given day every Jew was to be forced to sacrifice upon the pagan altars. When his agents sought to get the old priest Eleazar to do so, he refused. They pled with him simply to toss some incense into the altar fire, saying that because of his great influence the younger people would be willing to do likewise. Again he refused. Then they sought to get him to eat swine's flesh; again his refusal. Indignant, they sought to force him to swallow some. Each time he spit it out. Finally, they cut out his tongue, the organ with which he spoke his refusal. Finally he mounted the torture rack to die for his faith.

An even more horrible ordeal was that of a mother and her seven sons. When the first son refused to forsake his loyalty to Jehovah by eating swine's flesh, the agents cut out his tongue; then first one ear and then the other. With each repeated refusal they cut off his arms and legs, leaving only the torso. This they placed in a large pan over a fire and fried him alive. Throughout the ordeal his mother and brothers were exhorting him to be faithful to God, for God would raise him up in the resurrection. Then each son in turn, and finally the mother, suffered the same fate, in each case being exhorted to faithfulness. Each refused the temporal deliverance (cf. 2 Macc. 6:21ff.) in faith of a better resurrection.

Of all these the author says the world was not worthy (v. 38). Yet they persisted in their faith for, like Abraham, they looked for "a city which hath foundations, whose builder and maker is God."

3. The Expectation of the Faithful Under the New Covenant (vv. 39-40)

But all these despite their faithfulness did not receive *the promise* (v. 39). That they obtained promises is seen in 11:33, but they were only intermediate to the promise made to Abraham and his seed. Abel saw the significance of his sacrifice, but he did not live to see him who was God's once-for-all sacrifice. Enoch enjoyed fellowship with God, but it was far short of the visible presence of God in Jesus. Noah saw the promise in the rainbow, but it was not given to him to see the promise on Calvary. Abraham saw Jesus' day afar off and rejoiced, but he did not live to see that day at hand. Moses saw the passover in the paschal lamb, but he died without seeing in the flesh our Passover who was slain for us (1 Cor. 5:7).

Although the multitude of Old Testament worthies suffered and achieved within the eternal purpose of God, they did not live to see its ultimate fulfilment in Christ. All that they saw was but a shadow of the true promise which God had *foreseen* (provided) for the followers of Christ (v. 40*a*).

Because of this, it is all the more important that the Hebrew Christians, and Christians throughout the ages, should be faithful in their generation as were the heroes of faith in former days. For "they without us should not be made perfect" (v. 40). The line of faith must be unbroken, else all that went before was in vain. The word "perfected," we repeat, carries the idea of an intended end or goal. The faithful of the Old Testament endured as they saw the redemptive purpose of God running through the ages. Each generation must share its responsibility in carrying that purpose to its ultimately successful conclusion.

For Review and Further Study

1. What was the promise made to Abraham (Gen. 12:1-3)? What is the promise made to us?
2. What is the condition of God's promise to us? Has God kept his part of the covenant? Have we? What is the meaning of Hebrews 10:29?
3. What is the basis upon which we receive the promise? What is faith? Read Hebrews 11. How does our failure affect the heroes of faith?

9

MOTIVATED FOR SERVICE

[12:1 to 13:25]

THE CALL to Christian growth and service on the part
of Christian people is all the more pressing in the light
of the motive which presses them onward toward their
goal. For this reason their responsibility to God is all
the more compelling. That God waits upon his people
we have seen. Indeed, the unredeemed millions of the
earth wait upon us. The millions wait, God calls, and
his people must answer. The motive of yesteryears is the
present stimulus which calls for a response.

The word "therefore" is said by Dr. A. T. Robertson
to be a "triple compound inferential participle" and
is "a conclusion of emphasis." It refers back not only to
the thought which immediately precedes it, but includes
the entire evidence of the epistle. Coming to a final conclusion, therefore, the author presents in reverse but in
climaxing order the threefold inspiration which char-
acterizes the Christian's motive.

I. THE MOTIVE OF INSPIRATION (vv. 1-4)

1. The Inspiration of Former Triumphs (v. 1a)

"Seeing we also are compassed about with so great a
cloud of witnesses." We are called upon to look about
us at the great cloud of witnesses or martyrs. The word
"cloud" is used here only in the New Testament and
means a great mass of clouds. This metaphor is suggestive

of a vast arena surrounded by tier upon tier of seats rising up as a cloud. The author regards these witnesses (*martures*—note our word "martyr") not as mere spectators, else he would have used the word *theatai* (note our word "theater") which means just that. These are *testifiers* who out of their own experience can testify to the keeping power of God through all their trials.

It is clear that the heroes of faith mentioned in chapter 11 are the witnesses which the author has in mind. They, too, in their day faced sore trials in their efforts to fulfil their destiny in the purpose of God. But despite that fact they placed their trust in God and went on to victory. What they have done we can do. Our problems are no greater than those of our forefathers in the faith. The same God has promised to be with us even more definitely than he was with the faithful under the old covenant. From the experiences of those who had endured in the past we can take courage for the future.

2. *The Inspiration of a Great Purpose (v. 1b)*

"Let us run with patience the race that is set before us." The cloud of witnesses had a course to run, and they ran it to the end. But their running cannot suffice for others. The picture is that of a relay race. Those who have run have passed on to us the redemptive purpose of God which must be carried forward in our generation, at the end of which we, in turn, shall pass it on to others. The full course will not have been run until he who set it says that it is enough. Failure in any one of the relays can negate the valiant efforts of those who have gone before.

For that reason we are urged to do our best. In order to do this we must lay aside every weight. Track men often train in heavier shoes than those worn in the race. This enables them to be lighter on their feet, thus adding

to their efficiency in the race itself. We are called upon
to cast aside every handicap such as doubt, pride, lazi-
ness, or any other thing which will keep us from doing
our best. Furthermore, we are to lay aside "the sin which
doth so easily beset us." The true rendering is "the easily
besetting sin." Runners ran in the stadium almost naked.
They wore no cloak which might entangle and trip them.
The sin which we believe that the author has in mind,
as often before, is the sin of *standing off from* God in refusing to pursue his purpose for his people. It is ever
the *easily besetting sin* of every Christian generation both
individually and collectively. Having cast it aside, we are
to run the race with "patience." We have seen that this
word refers to rugged and positive endurance, not to
passive waiting.

3. *The Inspiration of Our Leader (vv. 2-4)*

"Looking unto Jesus." After a passing glance at the
witnesses we are to *look away* to Jesus. He is "the author
and finisher of our faith." The runner who gazes at the
crowd in the stands will do little to achieve the goal.
While mindful of their presence, he has eyes only for his
coach, the one for whom he runs. Jesus is the Pioneer
(forerunner) of our faith. He has gone before us to blaze
the way. He is the Perfecter (goal) of our faith. His own
faith in God persevered to the accomplishment of God's
purpose for him. As such he is our goal, in that in him
our faith shall also carry us forward to the realization of
the end for which we have been called. Elsewhere Jesus
has been called God's Son (1:2), our Brother (2:11), our
Apostle and High Priest (3:1), our Partner (3:14), the
Mediator (8:6), and our Sacrifice (9:14). Here he is
called the Pioneer and Perfecter of our faith. The same
general idea is present in all these titles, but the author
adjusts them to stress a particular relation in keeping

with the immediate thought involved. In this particular instance his uppermost thought is probably that of the Christian's part in the relay race of redemption from age to age.

The titles applied to Jesus at this time are most suggestive. In fact, they may be combined into the one idea involved in the word "coach." A coach is one who has formerly participated personally in the game, but who has finished his active participation as a player. Out of his own experience, therefore, he is able to develop and direct others as they participate in the contest. Even so, through them the coach is still an integrate and active participant in the race.

In his personal participation in the race of redemption Jesus "endured the cross, despising the shame, and is set down at the right hand of the throne of God." Crucifixion was the most painful and shameful of deaths. The pain was the excruciating agony of a slow death. The shame involved not only the jeers of the mob and the stigma of crime, but the victim was crucified stark naked. However, in the case of Jesus we have seen that the pain and shame involved more. It meant that sinless and pure though he was, he became the very essence of sin, that in his person he might endure the full wrath of God against sin. Yet he endured it because it was in keeping with the redemptive will of his Father. Having finished his *race*, he sat down at the right hand of the throne of God. All this he did "for the joy that was set before him." It was not the joy of sitting down or even of winning the race. His joy was in the fact that in so doing he was perfectly obedient to the will of God (John 5:30; cf. John 17:4), and that by his death he would achieve the full salvation of all who should trust in him (John 17:6, 20).

Because of this we are urged to "consider" him (v. 3;

cf. 3:1) lest "ye be wearied and faint in your minds."
Aristotle uses both these verbs (weary, faint) to describe
runners who relax and collapse once the goal has been
passed. Here the warning is that we cannot "relax" and
"collapse" *before* we have passed the goal. It is here that
our Coach must play his part. He knows the arduous
trial of the race. He himself had been tempted to *relax*
and *collapse* before his race was run. Therefore he knows
how to develop our skill and stamina and to pace us so
that we can run, and run to win.

The immaturity of the early Christians for the race
is seen in the fact that they "have not yet resisted unto
blood, striving against sin" (v. 4). The idea of resist
carries the picture of troops lined up face to face for
battle. The witnesses before him, and Jesus himself, have
stood face to face with the powers of evil. Tempted
though they were to *stand off from* God's purpose in
destroying the power of the prince of this world, still
they *slugged it out* with sin unto the death. While these
Christian people have not done so, they are to *analogize*
(consider) Jesus as one who has, and who can enable
them to do so. He is their, and our, supreme inspiration
and motive in remaining true to God's purpose for his
people.

II. The Motive of Relationship (vv. 5-29)

Passing from this potent thought, the author reminds
us that we should persevere because of the relationship
which we bear. As our inspiration is threefold, so do we
bear a threefold relationship which ties us to our task.

1. *Our Relationship as Sons of God (vv. 5-11)*

We are to remain steadfast in God's purpose because,
unlike Moses who was a servant in God's house (3:5),
we, like Jesus, bear the relation of sonship (3: 6). Jesus

is the Son of God; we have *become* sons of God (John 1: 12). As such Jesus is not ashamed to call us brethren (2:11). Therefore since we are sons, we should not behave like hirelings (John 10:12), but should follow our elder Brother in considering our Father's business as our own (John 14:10).

This relationship as sons of God is the very basis of every Christian's present trials. Because we are God's children, the world hates us (John 15:19). This truth the author seizes upon by quoting from Proverbs 3:1-12: "My son, despise not thou [regard not lightly] the chastening of the Lord, nor faint [relax] when thou art rebuked of him: . . ." The word "to chasten" is a Greek word meaning *to train a child,* and should be so translated throughout this passage. The word "rebuked" in Alexandrian Judaism is the term used for an appeal to a person to rise to the higher philosophy of life (Conybeare). Thus the present afflictions of the Hebrew Christians are but a training and an appeal for them to rise to a greater life of service. Not that God himself actually sends these things upon his people, but he allows them to come, and will use them for their training, if they will only regard them in that light (v. 7).

Christian people often wonder why they are caused to suffer for certain actions, while others, doing the same things, apparently escape the consequences. It is because the former is a son of God while the other is not (v. 8). Even earthly fathers train their children, sometimes whipping them in the process, but it is an act of love (v. 6). Should not God be expected to do as much (v. 9)? But while the training may be grievous at the time, it is for our own "profit" that we might become more in the image of God as we share in his holiness. The word "holiness" suggests God's own dedication to his redemptive purpose in which we are to share (v. 10). This is all to the end that we might attain unto "the peaceable [after the training is over] fruit of righteousness unto them which are exercised thereby" (v. 11). The word "exercised" comes from the Greek word *gumnazo* which refers to a state of completion which comes from the discipline of a gymnasium. Thus the author ties together the entire section (vv. 1-11) under the thought of training for "the race that is set before us."

2. Our Relationship to One Another (vv. 12-17)

Because we are all members of the family of God, we have a responsibility to ourselves and to one another in seeing to it that no one fails in his Christian growth and service. Therefore we are to see to it that no one grows weary in the race, so that his hands droop (hold up one another's hands) or his legs grow limp (v. 12). We are to be sure that we run on a straight and even track, lest some being made lame stumble and fall out of the course (v. 13). If such does happen to one, we are to heal him that he might run again (cf. 2 Cor. 2:6ff.). We are to avoid the strife which sometimes arises even through our zeal to win the race. Instead we are to be wholly dedicated (meaning of "holiness") to the task that at the end of the course we may see God waiting to congratulate us and to give to us the rest we have earned (v. 14). We are to exercise oversight over one another lest any should *fall short* of the grace of God as seen in his promise that we shall enter into the rest of his world redemptive purpose (4:1). To fall short is to be defiled, making us unfit for fellowship with Christ in service (v. 15).

In short, there is to be among us no profane person like Esau, who for a temporary satisfaction sold his part in the redemptive plan of God (v. 16). Even though later he earnestly desired to receive it again, he could not. His tears of regret were insufficient to enable him to change his mind or attitude (root meaning of *repentance*), so that he would be a fit instrument in God's hands for divine service (v. 17). Even so, we, too, shall suffer if for the safety and ease of a meaningless Christian life we forfeit the opportunities of this present moment. We have only one life in which to serve God. The tears of old age cannot undo the failures of our youth. How we need to heed this warning!

3. *Our Relationship in a Divine Mission (vv. 18-29)*

Furthermore, our motive is rooted in a divine mission which is expressed in a new covenant. Ours is not a mission which was sealed among the fires and thunderings of Mount Sinai (vv. 18-21; cf. Ex. 19:16; Deut. 9:19). Our covenant is sealed in Mount Zion, the heavenly Jerusalem (cf. Gal. 4:21-31), wherein is an innumerable company of angels, and the company of the redeemed (the kingdom of God), and God the Judge of all, and the spirits of Old Testament saints whose justification has now been perfected, and Jesus who is the Mediator of our new covenant, whose blood has been sprinkled, and which speaks more eloquently than the blood of Abel (vv. 22-24). This is but a summary of the author's foregoing argument as to the superiority of our covenant over the old.

For that reason we are not to refuse to fulfil the condition of our covenant. If they failed to escape the consequences of their refusal, how can we expect to escape if we refuse the one who has entered into a covenant relation with us? The one who shook Mount Sinai has said that he will shake heaven and earth in the accomplishment of his purpose (vv. 25-26; cf. Hag. 2:6f.). The world to which we cling is transitory, but the kingdom of God remains (v. 27). Therefore let us forsake the glamor and ease of the world and fit ourselves into the program of

God's kingdom. Having received this eternal kingdom, let us keep on having grace (or gratitude, as the word probably means here, cf. Luke 17: 9), by which we may continue to serve God with reverence and godly fear, and in a manner well pleasing to him (v. 28). Let us exercise caution lest we forget the covenant of our Lord, which he has made with us, "for our God is a consuming fire" (v. 29; cf. Deut. 4:23f.), and is not to be trifled with.

III. THE MOTIVE OF CONVICTION (13:1-19)

To do this we must be a people of conviction. This is no mere skirmish in which we are engaged, but a war to the finish. It is no place for reeds shaken with the wind, or for lounge lizards who wear soft raiment and live in king's houses (Matt. 11: 7-9).

> Henceforth in fields of conquest
>   Thy tents shall be our home.
> Thro' days of preparation
>   Thy grace has made us strong,
> And now, O King Eternal,
>   We lift our battle song.
>
> —ERNEST W. SHURTLEFF

1. The Conviction of Personal Purity (vv. 1-7)

If we continue in our God-given destiny, our hearts must be filled with love both for our brethren and for strangers (vv. 1-2). We are to be mindful of our compatriots who suffer for the cause of Christ, knowing that we also may be called upon to do the same (v. 3). Our home life must be above reproach (v. 4). Knowing that the love of money is the root of all evil, our whole manner of life (conversation) must be free from covetousness (v. 5). Our first concern must be not for self but for the cause of Christ, relying always upon him not only to provide for our needs, but to keep us from the evil which men do to us as we try to serve him (v. 6). Furthermore, we must be mindful of the leadership of those who have been divinely commissioned to teach us and to lead us on in the service of Christ. We must imitate their faith, that together we may achieve the purpose to which their lives are dedicated (v. 7).

2. *The Conviction of Sound Doctrine (vv. 8-15)*

We must fix our faith upon Christ. "Jesus Christ is the same yesterday, and to day, yea and for ever" (v. 8 ASV). Therefore, he was sufficient for the trials of those who went before us; he is sufficient for our present problems; and he will be sufficient through all ages to come. Furthermore, he is our eternal message as God's remedy for sin. With our faith fixed in him, we shall not be carried about by every strange doctrine which comes along (v. 9). Now, as then, there are many devilish doctrines which would deter us in our divine purpose. To avoid these we are to have our hearts established in the gospel of grace, not in the mere external rites and ceremonies of religion.

We are not to be ashamed of Christ or his redemption by blood (vv. 10-15). Instead, we are to share the reproach which sinful men place upon him. As the sin offering of Judaism was burned outside the camp as being unfit for human consumption, so was Christ crucified outside the gate of Jerusalem. But we are not to let him bear his cross of shame alone while we go free. Rather let us offer our sacrifice of praise as with our lips we continue to confess his name.

3. *The Conviction of Co-operative Service (vv. 16-19)*

In our service for Christ we are to seek always to do good (v.16a). Furthermore, we are to contribute our money (communicate, cf. 2 Cor. 9:13) to the ongoing of his work, for such is pleasing to God (v.16b). Again we are reminded to submit ourselves obediently in co-operative service unto those who are appointed as our guides in service (vv. 16f.). They are conscientious in their sleepless watching over our spiritual welfare. This is so because they realize that they must give an account of their leadership. We should so conduct ourselves that they may lead us in joy and not in grief. For our own welfare depends upon this co-operative endeavor.

The writer closes his exhortation by requesting that they pray for him that he might have a good conscience in that he shall live honestly (v.18). Apparently unworthy motives have been attributed to him. What Christian leader could not make this request! However, his main purpose in requesting prayer is that he may be restored to them sooner than he expects. It is possible that he was ill (Robertson), and, therefore, requests their prayers.

IV. BENEDICTION AND PERSONAL MATTERS (vv. 20-25)

1. *Personal Matters (vv. 22-25)*

Shifting the order of this passage, we look into the heart of the author as he adds a postscript. He begs his readers to accept his exhortation in the same manner that he gives it (v. 22). He tells them that his brother, Timothy, is now a free man, and together they hope to visit them shortly (v. 23). Greetings are sent to their leaders and to all the congregation from both the author and the Christians who reside in Italy (v. 24). With a prayer for grace to abide with them, he closes this timely but timeless letter (v. 25).

2. *Benediction (vv. 20-21)*

Let us allow the author to pronounce upon us all one of the most beautiful benedictions found in Holy Writ:

"Now the God of peace, that brought again from the dead our Lord Jesus, that great shepherd of the sheep, through the blood of the everlasting covenant, make you perfect in every good work to do his will, working in you that which is wellpleasing in his sight, through Jesus Christ; to whom be glory for ever and ever. Amen."

FOR REVIEW AND FURTHER STUDY

1. List the threefold elements of our inspiration to faithfulness. Who are the *witnesses*? What is the significance of the titles *author* and *finisher*?
2. Are you a son of God? What is the purpose of God's chastening?
3. Name the threefold conviction necessary for our Christian service. What should be our attitude toward those who lead us in our world mission?
4. Read Hebrews 13:20-21.

SYE
MARVIN
BERL
JOHNNIE S.